Dragons Drawing

Step by Step Guide

By Jong Mac

Copyright©2015 Jong Mac

Table of Contents

Disclaimer

While all attempts have been made to verify the information provided in this book, the author does assume any responsibility for errors, omissions, or contrary interpretations of the subject matter contained within. **The information provided in this book is for educational and entertainment purposes only. The reader is responsible for his or her own actions and the author does not accept any responsibilities for any liabilities or damages, real or perceived, resulting from the use of this information.**

The trademarks that are used are without any consent, and the publication of the trademark is without permission or backing by the trademark owner. All trademarks and brands within this book are for clarifying purposes only and are the owned by the owners themselves, not affiliated with this document.

Introduction

Dragons are mythical beings that never cease to capture the imagination. Many of us have read tales of fire-breathing dragons that kidnap fair maidens and destroy entire towns with their fiery breath. This is the European/Greek version of the fictional creature. In the east in countries such as China, the dragon takes on a different appearance and significance. The term dragon comes from the Latin word, 'draconem' and means 'a serpent of huge size'. There is also a Greek term, 'drakon' which means 'serpent'.

Most of the time, when we think of dragons, we think of a creature that is reptilian in nature. Often, it is covered in scales and has a long, serpent-like body. The idea of a dragon that has bat-like wings comes from the Middle Ages in Europe. Older versions of the mythological beast are more like a serpent. With time, the creature became more lizard-like. The Epic of Gilgamesh is the first writing that depicts a dragon as a destructive monster that is slain by a heroic figure.

Old European works of literature such as Beowulf began depicting dragons as fire-breathing beings or as poisonous creatures. This popular view of the creature has lingered into modern works of literature and modern feature films, such as *The Hobbit* by Tolkien. This popular work and major motion picture depict the dragon, Smaug, as a greedy villain who stole treasure form the dwarves and destroyed a neighboring town with his fire-breathing capabilities. Also, the popular television series, Game of Thrones continues the European tradition of depicting dragons as destructive, fire-breathing creatures.

Interestingly, the eastern view of the dragon is quite different form the western view. For one, the Chinese dragon is more serpent-like, often depicted without legs. This version of the dragon dates all the way back to the sixteenth century B.C. Dragons are considered to be a representation of the forces of nature and are often worshipped as beings that have inherent wisdom. In addition, they are symbols of longevity and are associated with water and sources of water, such as wells. In Chinese culture, the dragon represents power and was associated with the emperor.

The dragon is a symbol that exists in many cultures besides those of Europe and China. Versions of it exist in Indian, Persian, Vietnamese, and Japanese culture as well. The origins of the mythical being may indeed be based on actual animals that possess dragon-like qualities. The Nile crocodile and the spitting cobra are two animals that could have inspired the legend. Also, the komodo dragon of Indonesia has many dragon-like characteristics. Whatever the origin in the natural world, the dragon is a potent symbol in many cultures form around the world.

The sketching of dragons can be great for honing your technique as an artist. The remainder of this book will be a step-by-step guide with illustrations to show you an effective way to sketch dragons, one step at a time. By the time you are done reading this guide, you will be able to sketch six different examples of dragons. Hopefully this guide will provide you with guidelines that will make you a more competent artist. Grab your sketchpad and pencils; and enjoy your dragon-sketching experience

-

Chapter 1 – 'Side-view' Dragon

This is a dragon with the classic European/ Greek features that we have come to equate with the dragon. As with the dragons of old, it has reptilian qualities, four legs like a lizard and sharp teeth, giving it a vicious appearance. The tall horns give it an ominous look that it is common with many European depictions.

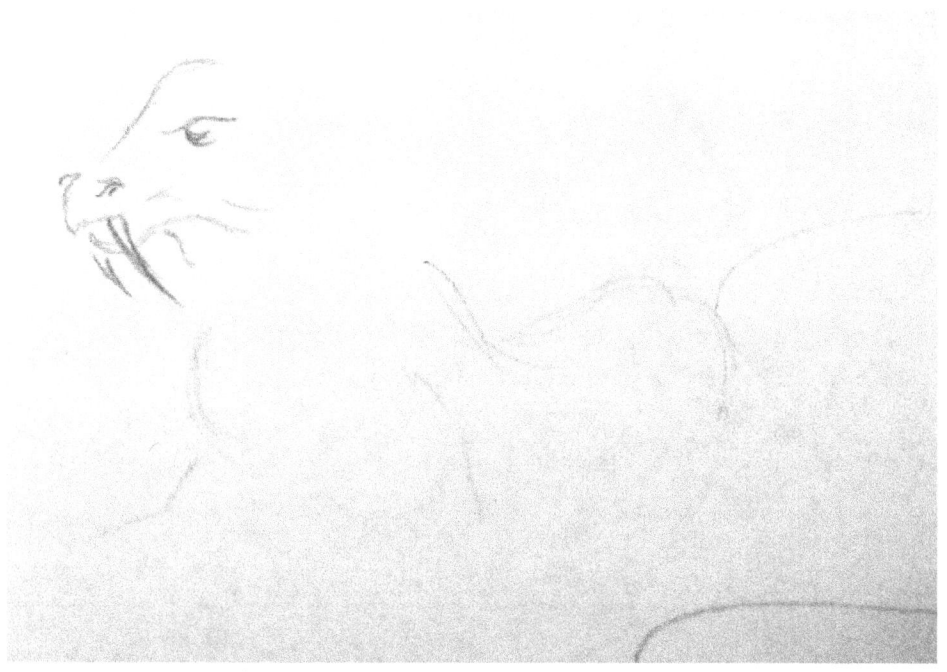

Drawing #1- The first step is to draw the outline of the head with a curved line to represent its forehead. Draw the fangs and nostrils, saving the finer details for later. Also, position the eye less than an inch below the top of its head. At this stage, you also want to put in a few broad strokes that will make up the chest, legs and back of the dragon. These should be very soft strokes of the pencil at this stage. Also include one curvy line that will later become the tail.

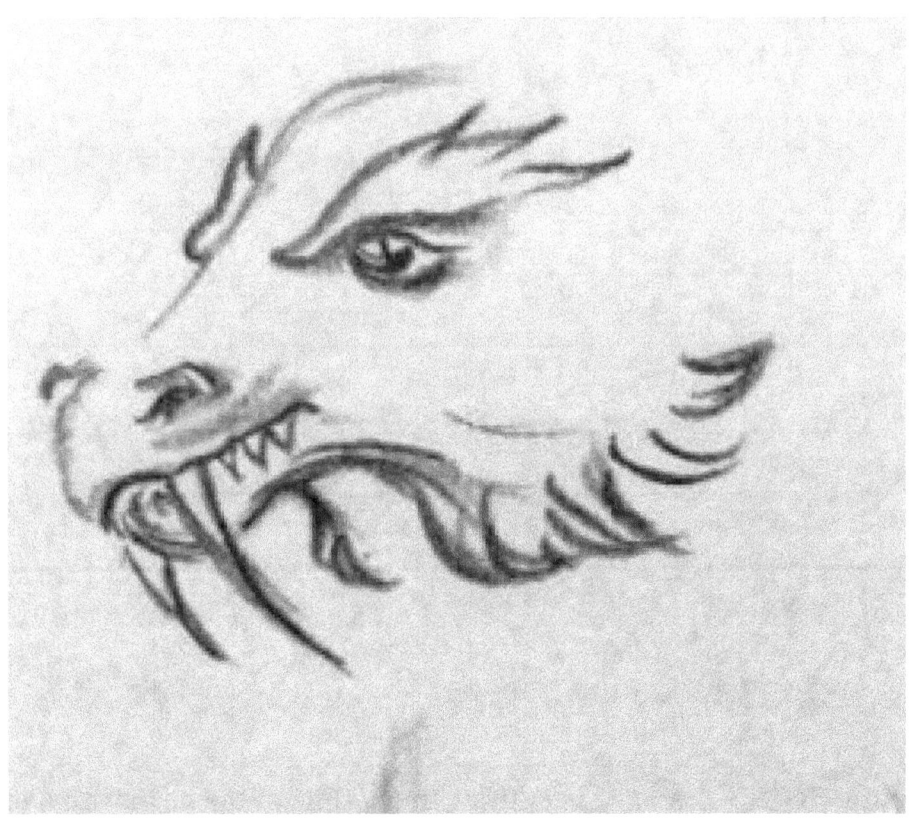

Drawing #2: Once you have a general outline of the face, it's time to add more detail. With darker stokes of the pencil add prominent eyebrows above the eyes. Complete the drawing of the eye with two rows of dark shading underneath them. Also, add some shading above the mouth and give your dragon some smaller teeth. Then, you should add some ruffles around the bottom of your dragon's neck using darker strokes.

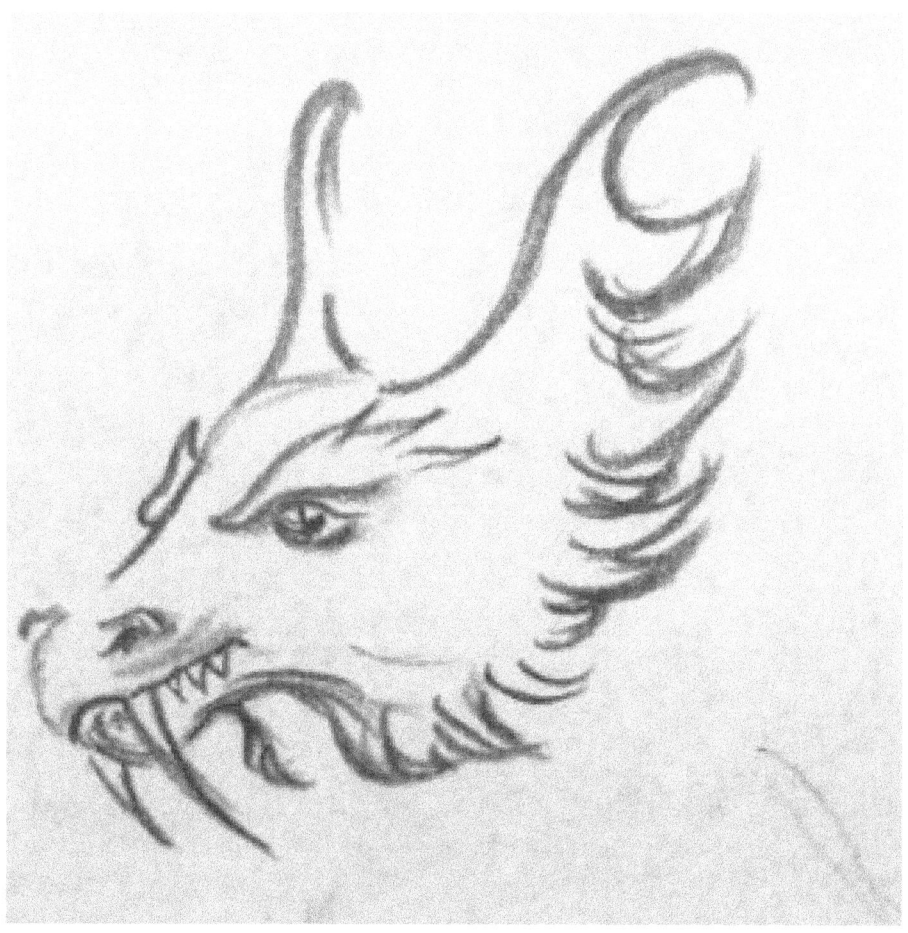

Drawing #3- At this stage, you want to complete the outline of the dragon's head, giving it horn-like structures on the top of its head and more ruffles connecting with the ruffles you added previously. Again, these should be dark, broad strokes that will allow this part of the dragon to stand out and provide some contrast.

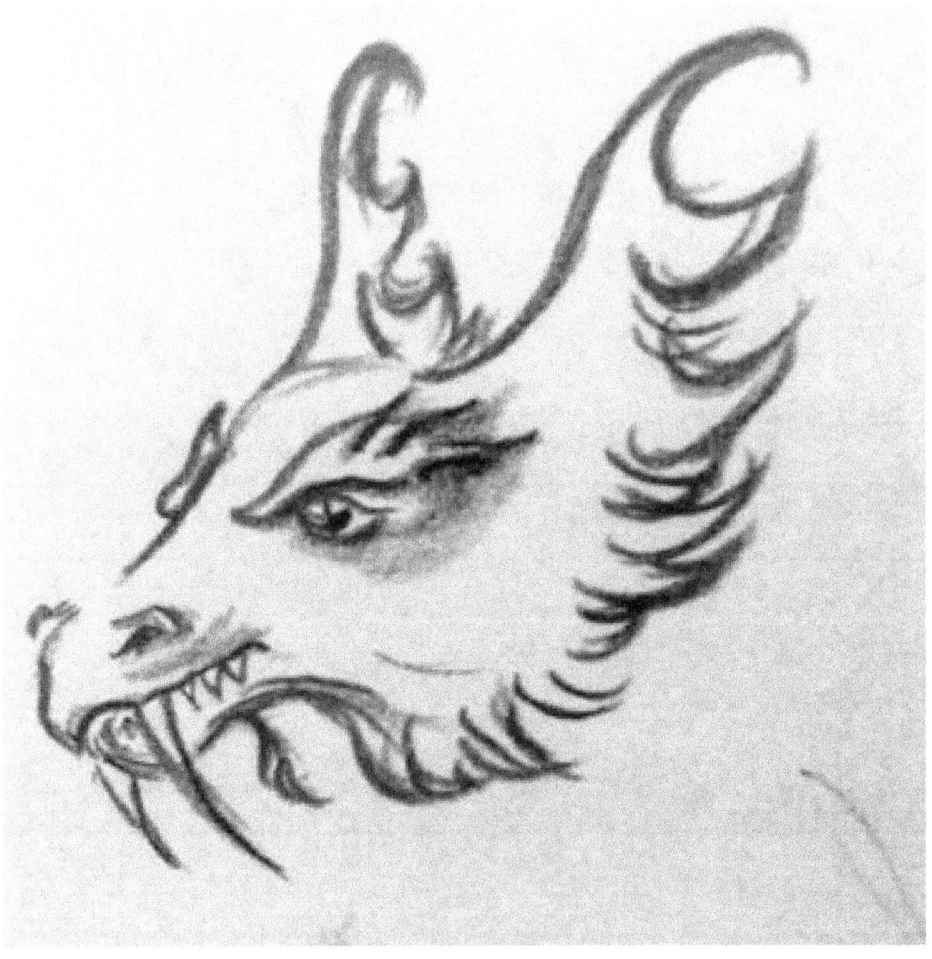

Drawing #4- Add some shading underneath the eye/eyebrow of the dragon by using the side of your pencil lead rather than the tip.

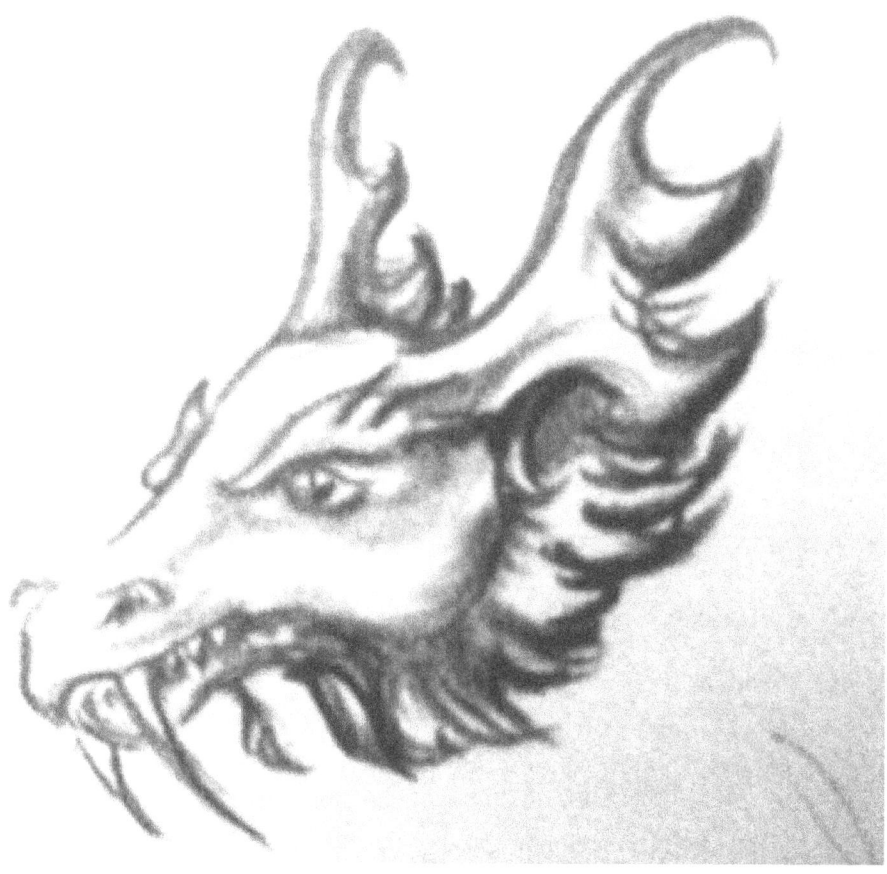

Drawing # 5- Complete the outline of the jaw using very broad, dark strokes of the pencil. Then, make a very dark rounded mark to indicate the dragon's ear opening. Also, add some light shading from the right nostril and up around the eye to create some contrast. Add some very dark strokes along the ruffles that extend beneath the jaw of the dragon. Add more of the same very dark strokes around the horns of the dragon with some sections of lighter shading through the mid-section of the dragon's horns.

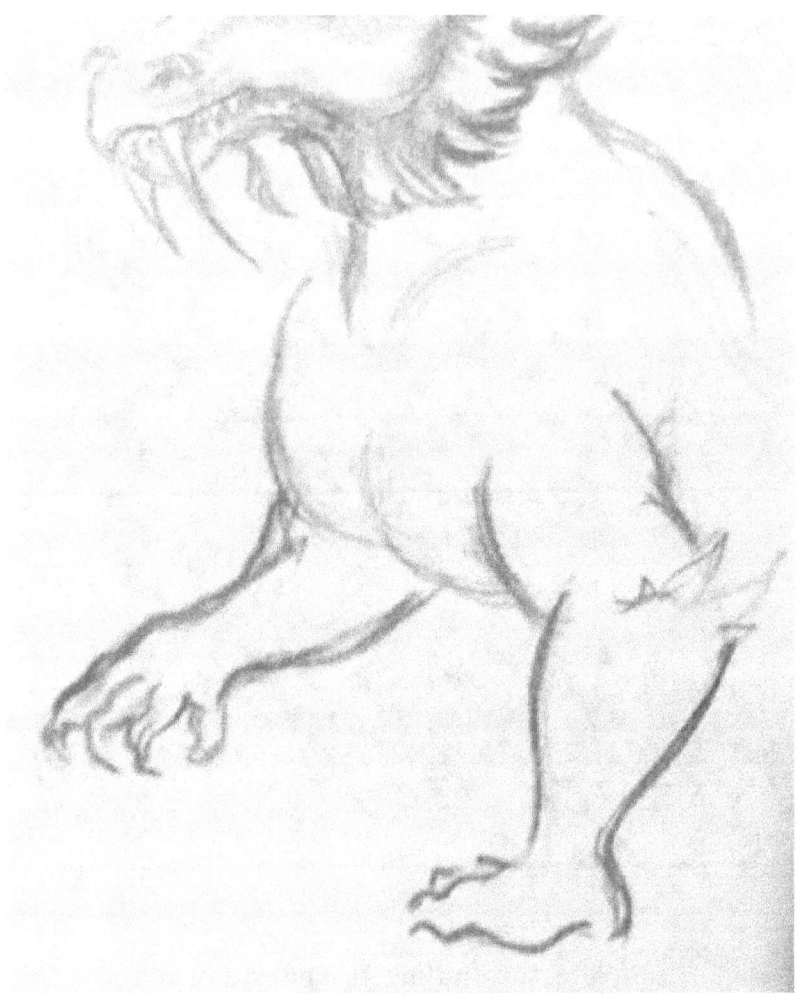

Drawing #6- Now, it's time to add the two front legs to your drawing. Use fairly dark strokes to make this part and add a chest with slighter lighter strokes and a broken line in the center of the chest to show a muscular structure. Add a few triangular spikes on the right front leg. Notice how the right foot is drawn to look like a side view and the left leg is lifted up slightly.

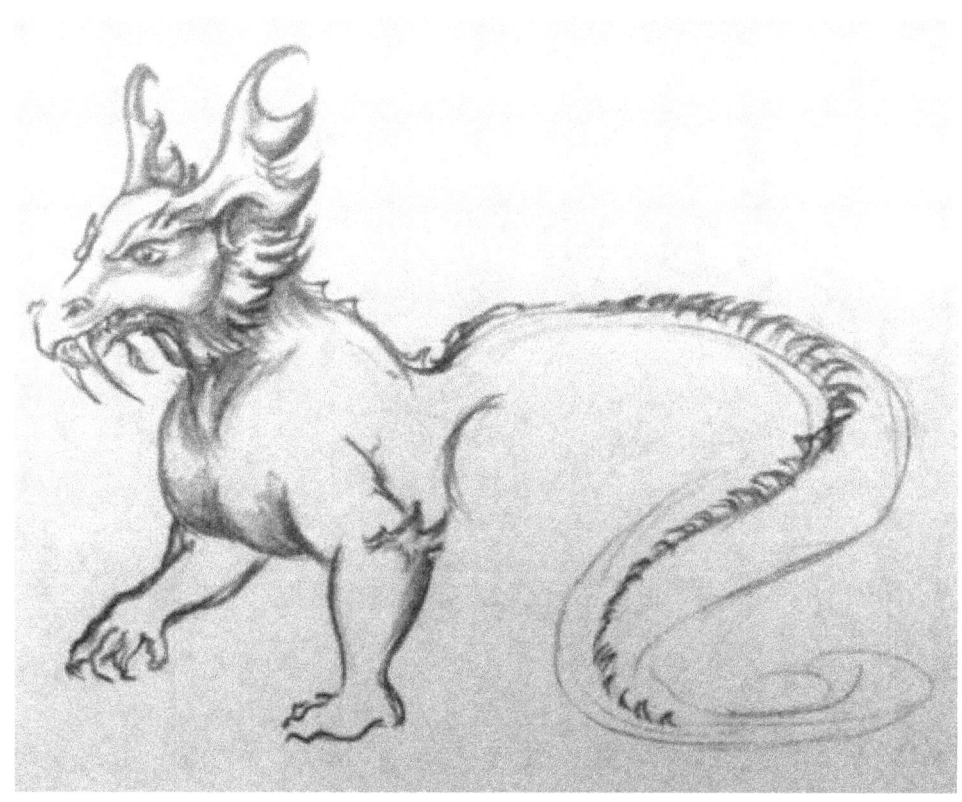

Drawing #7- Next, add some shading on the bottom portion of the chest and neck for contrast and begin to add the basic shape to the tail. Ad triangular spikes that extent all of the way form the dragon's head to the tip of the tail.

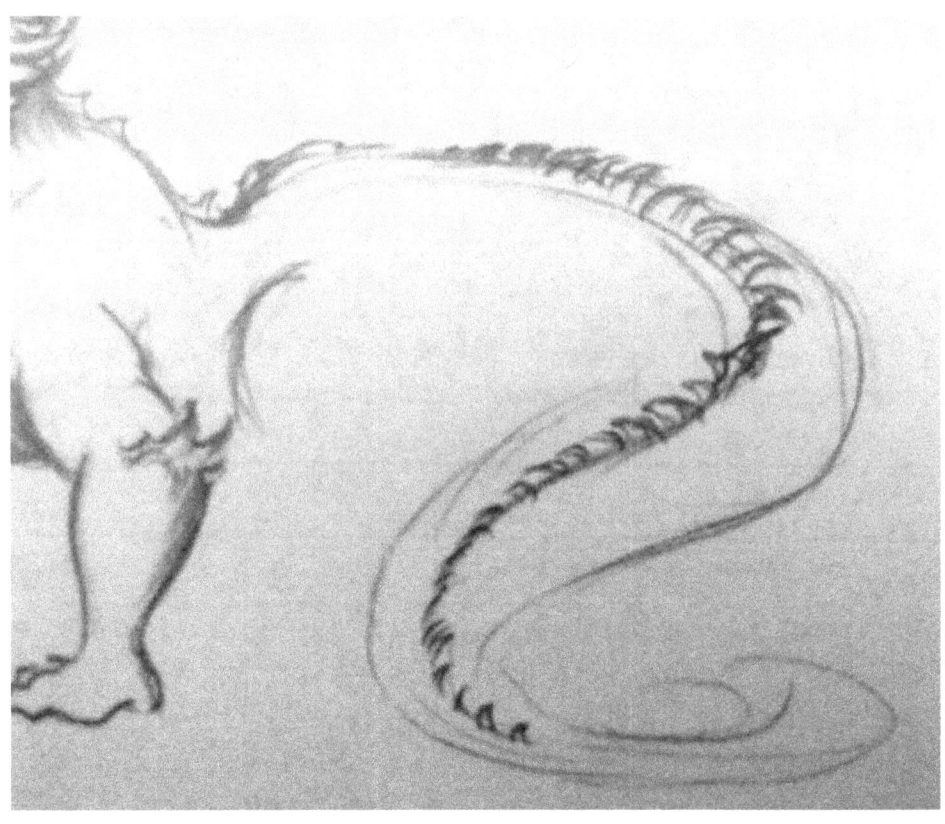

Drawing #8- Here's a close-up of the spikes that should be added on the tail. Notice how the spikes should be bolder and darker strokes than the outline of the tail.

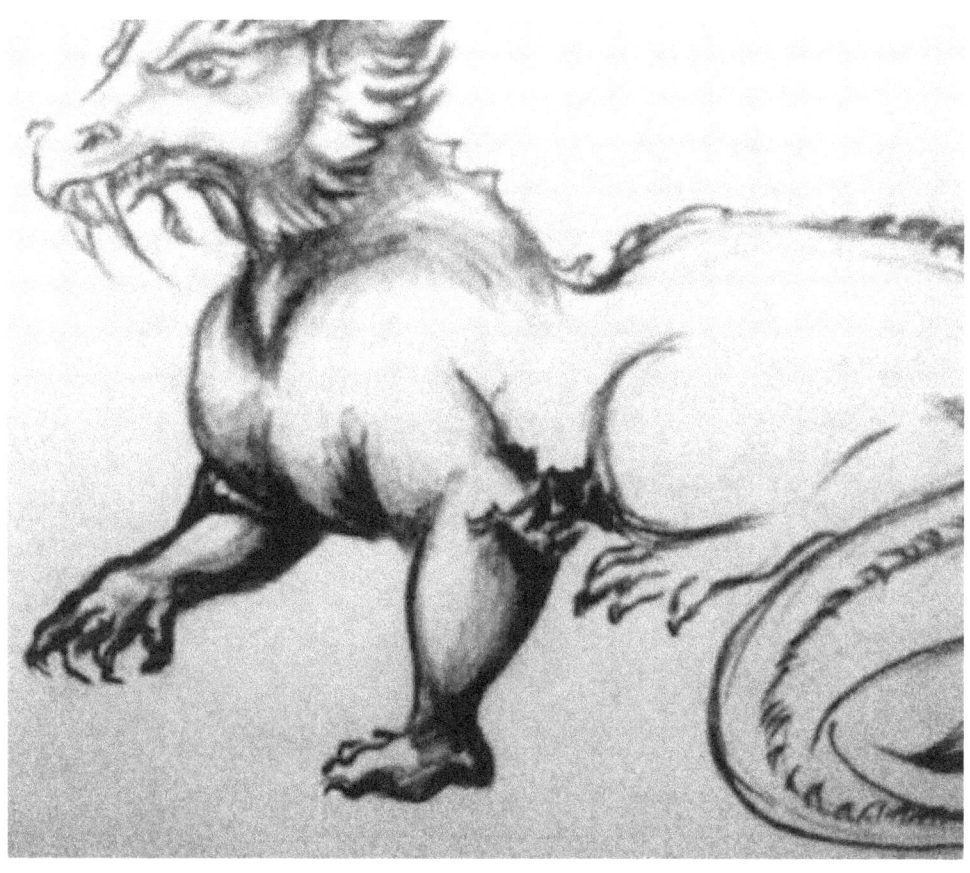

Drawing #9- At this stage, you need to add some much darker shading to the lower chest, 'v' shaped formation around the neck, and the outline and bottom portion of the front legs. This will be sure to add some dramatic contrast that will give your drawing some dramatic effect.

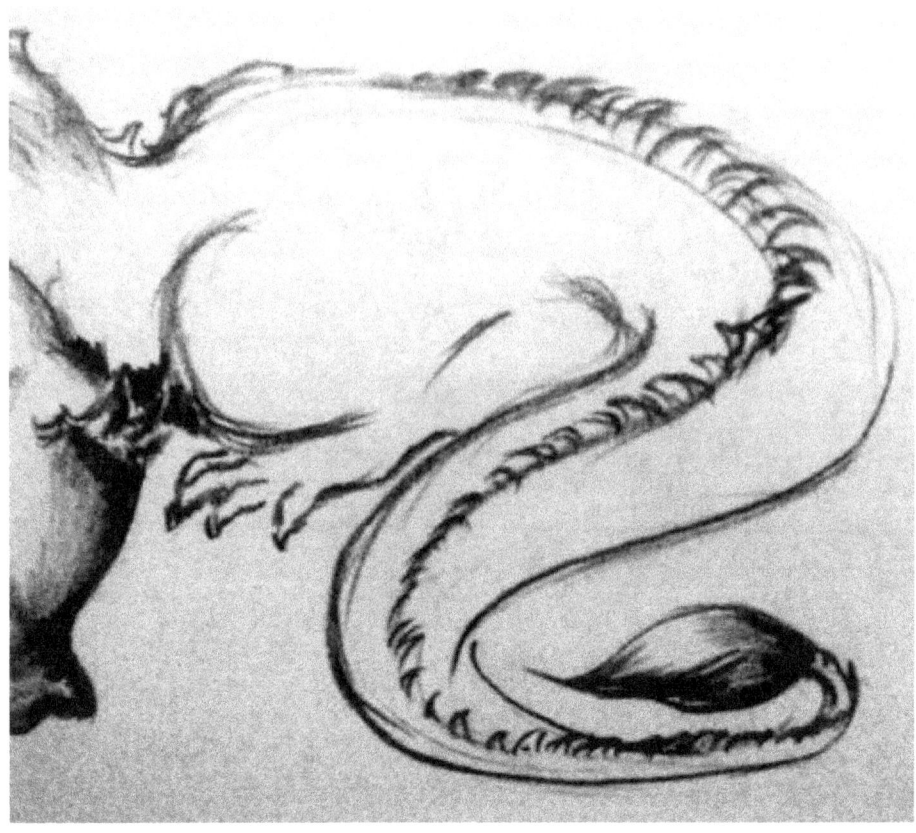

Drawing #10- Now, add the animals' hind leg with some dark strokes and add some darker, broader lines to the dragon's tail over the lighter marks you made earlier. Also, add the tuft-like structure on the end of the tail using darker strokes along the bottom and right portions of the tuft and a few lighter strokes of the pencil towards the middle.

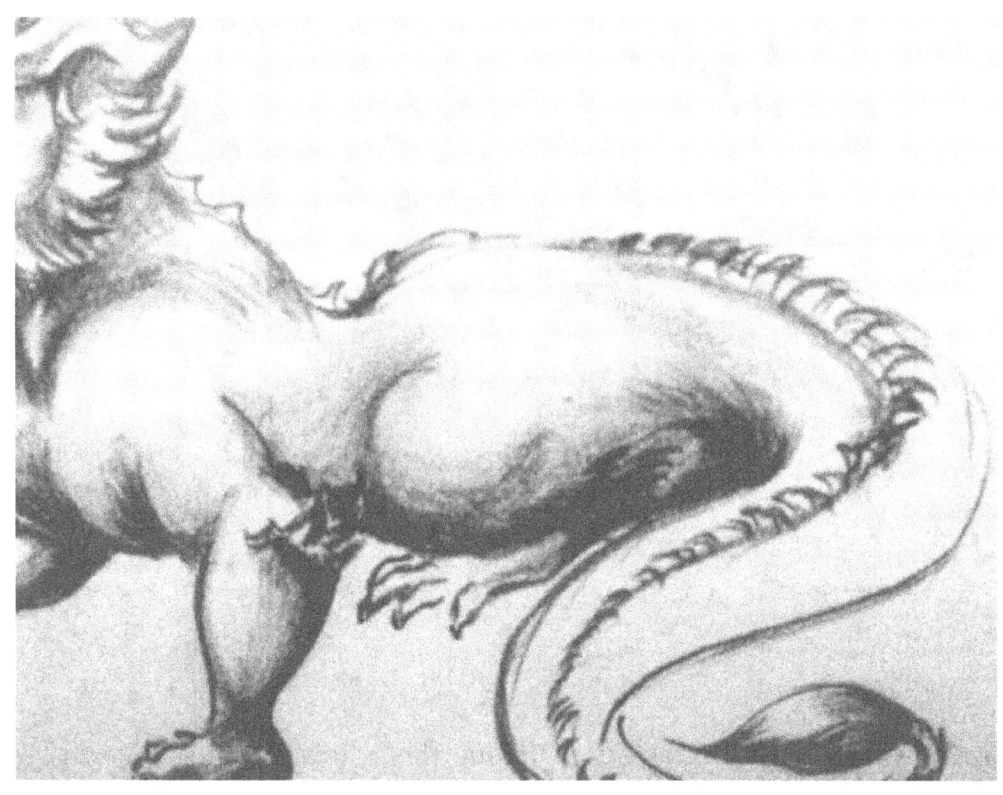

Drawing #11- Next, add some darker strokes along the portion of the hind leg that connects with the tail. Add some lighter shading just above the darker shading you drew. Also, add this lighter shading in between the front leg and the hind leg; and at the base of the tail. Again, the reason for this is to add texture and contrast to the drawing.

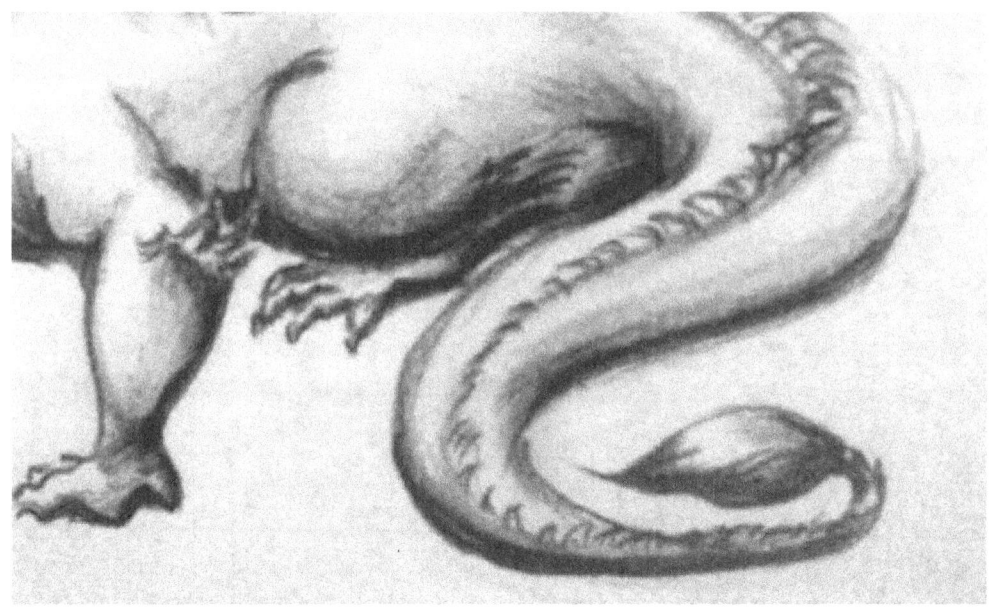

Drawing #12- This is a wider view of the dragon to show you how your drawing should have darker marks along the bottom of the dragon's body and lighter marks through the central portion of the dragon's body. Think of your drawing as if there was a light source shining on the top of the drawing with the bottom portion cast more in darker shadows.

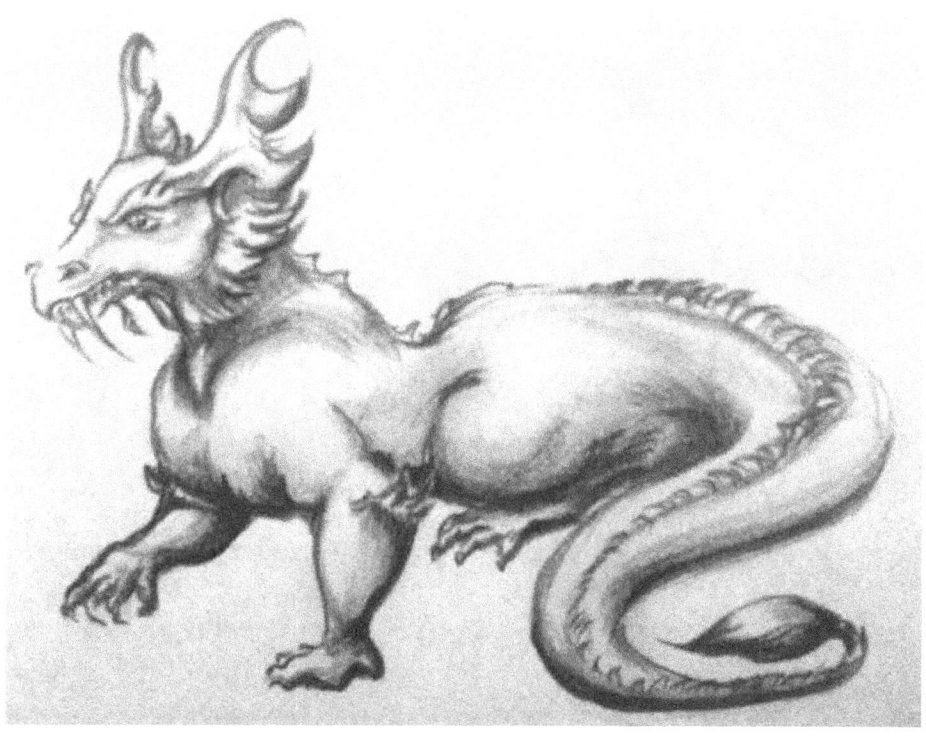

Drawing #13- Here is a full view of what you should have drawn so far.

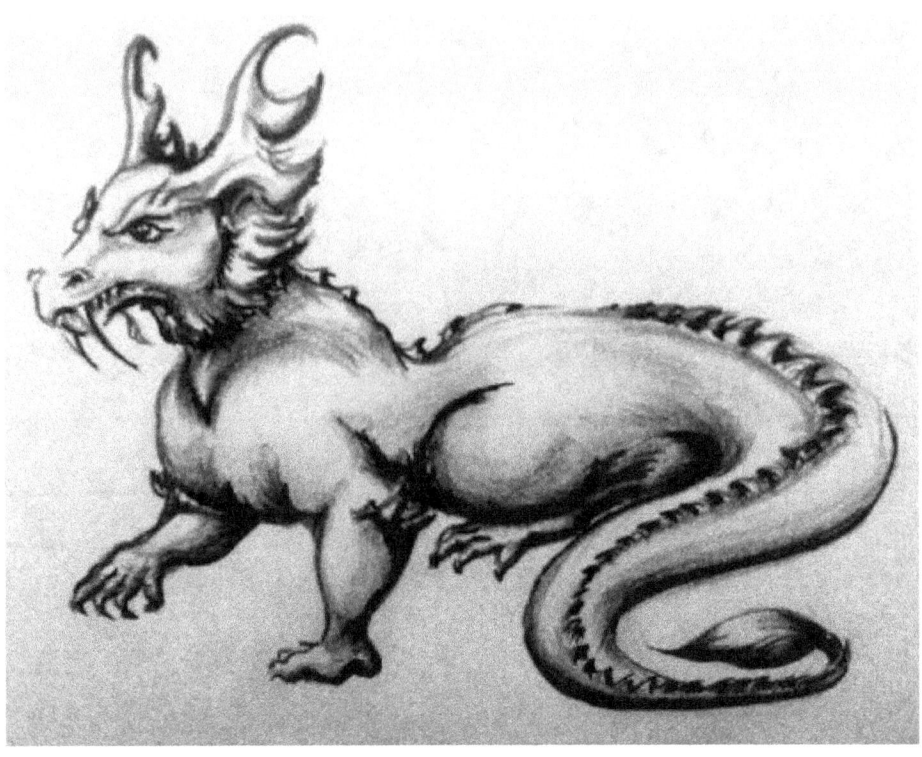

Drawing #14- Here, you should add even darker shading along the bottom of the neck ruffles, the base of the belly, the edges of the legs; and the region of the dragon's body where the front leg comes close to the rear leg. Again, the purpose is to add even more dramatic contrast to your drawing.

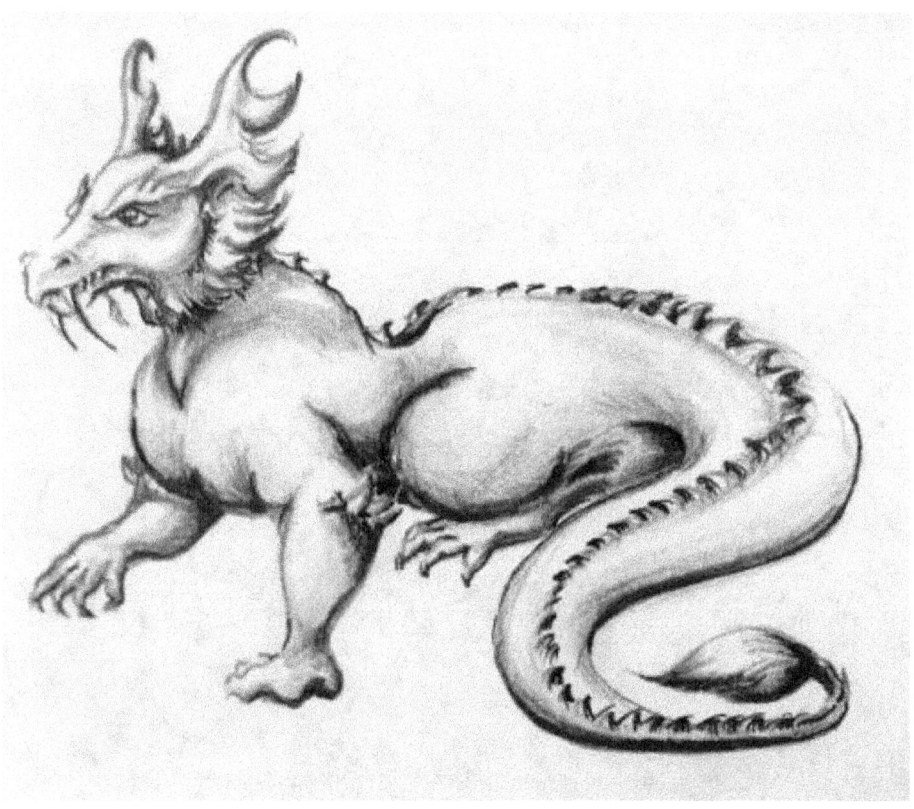

Drawing #15- At this stage, you need to add a few strokes using the side of the pencil lead to the portions of the dragon's body, below the neck, through the middle section of the body; and along the bottom portion of the front legs, rear leg; and where the rear leg come s close to the tail.

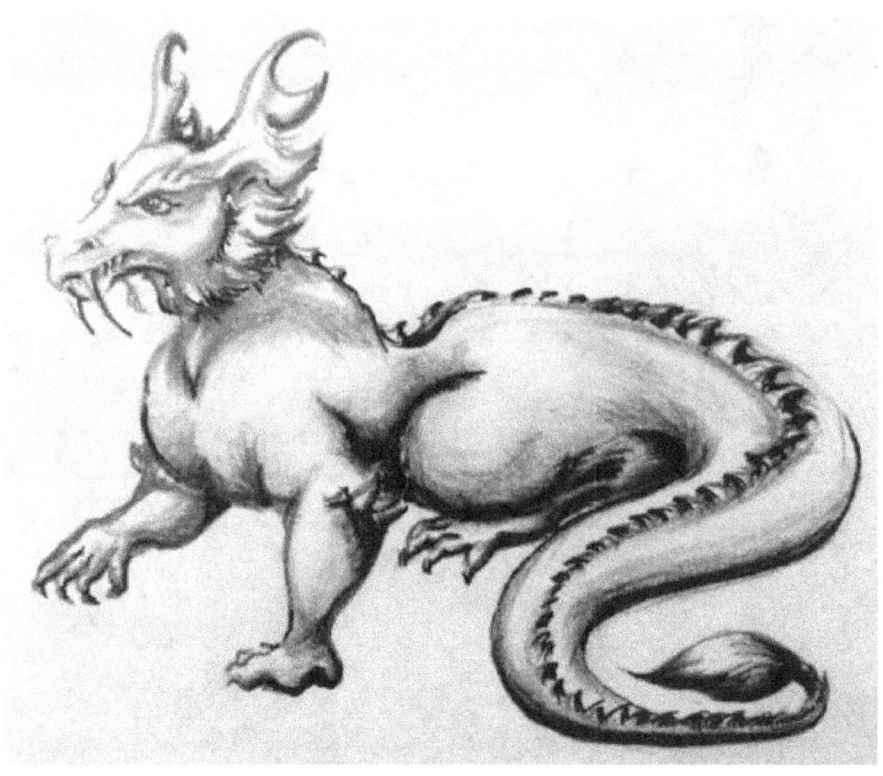

Drawing #16- At this last stage, add even more dark shading on the bottom portions of the dragon's body to further emphasize the contrast between the middle portion of the body and the edges. Now you have completed your first dragon!

Chapter 2 – 'Legless' Dragon:

Usually, the legless, dragon is more of an eastern symbol. It is more serpent-like in nature, rather than a lizard-like creature that walks on four legs. This one has some traits of the European depiction as well, however, with its long horns and fangs. It has a look in its eyes as if it is ready to stalk and hunt its prey.

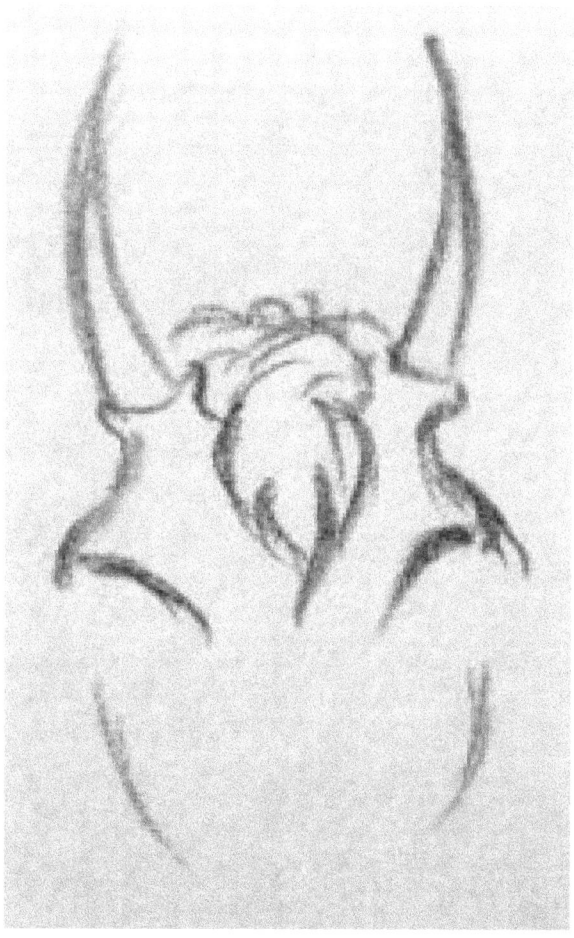

Drawing #1- Begin by drawing two horns about an inch apart from one another. Add a hairy 'tuft' in between the two horns that extends into the middle of its face. Add two darker strokes that will become the outline of the eye and two lighter marks that will make up the lower outline of the dragon's face.

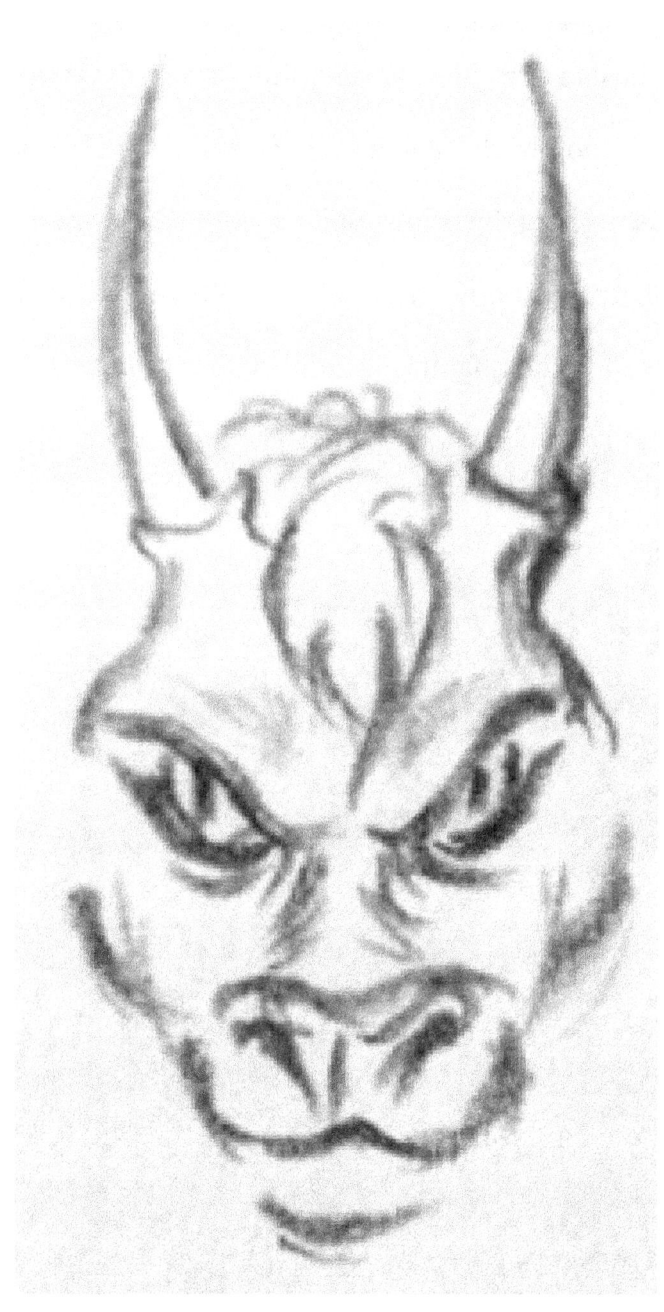

Drawing #2- Complete the eyes of the dragon with darker shading along the edges and slit-like eyes. Add shaded lines to the first two that you made to give more definition to the shape of its face. From the eyes, make a series of rippled marks to show the bridge of its nose. Then, draw a wide, 'm' shape with cow-like nostrils underneath the bridge of the nose. Also add a dark, 'w' shaped mark with some shading around it that will be the mouth of the dragon, along with a thick-shaded mark that will be the chin of the animal.

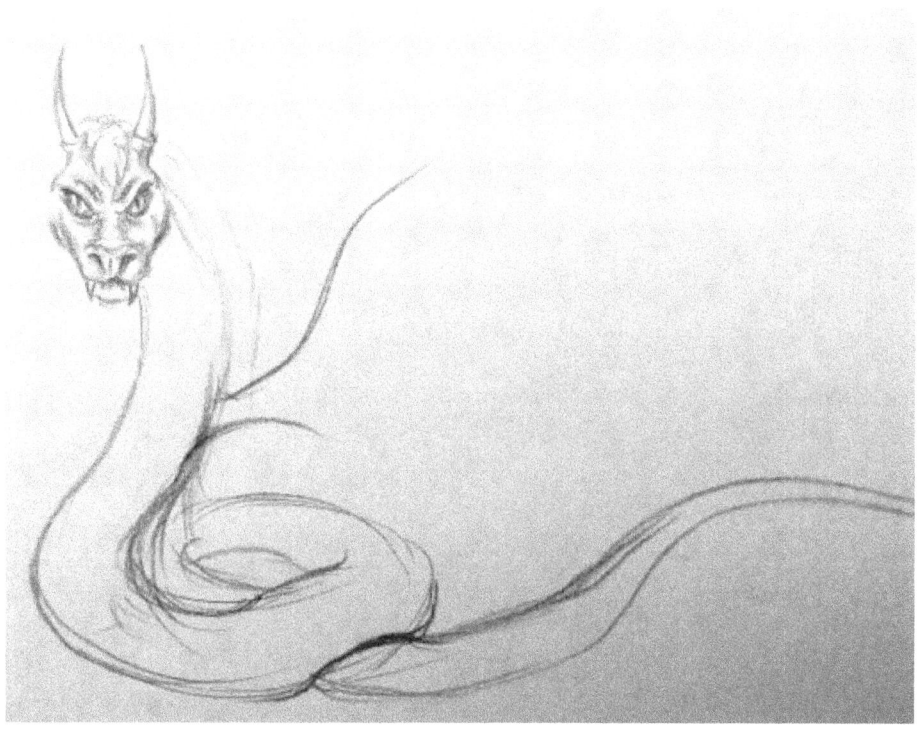

Drawing #3- Give your dragon two fangs extending from its mouth and more shading around the outline of its face. Also, give it some darker shaded marks above the eyes for eyebrows. Next, give your dragon a long, curved body that is snake-like. Its body should make a coil and then extend upwards into a tail.

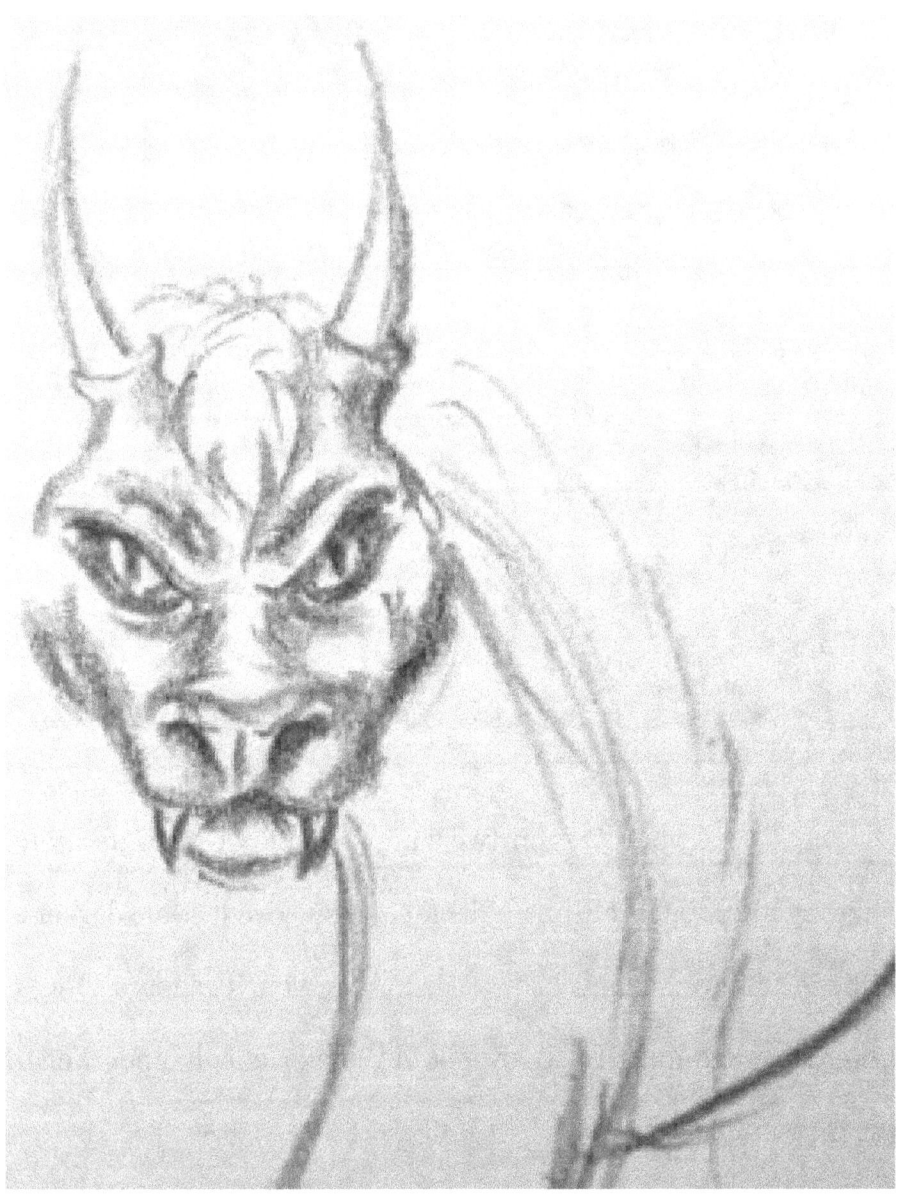

Drawing #4- Here is a close-up shot of the head. Notice the darker shading along the upper part of the eye, the nostrils, mouth, and along the right edge of its face. Lighter shading should be used along its nose, the bridge of the nose and extending forms the darker edges.

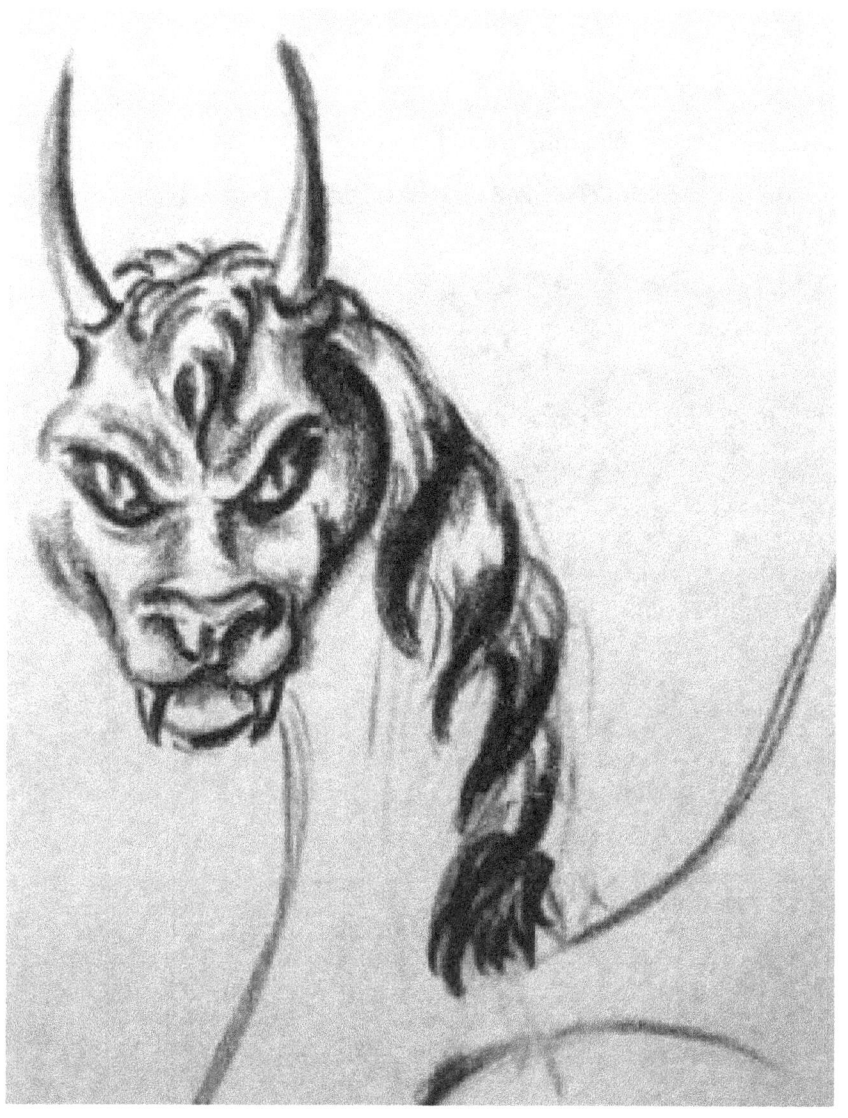

Drawing #5- Add some thick lines along the right side of the dragon's neck with darker shading along the bottom of each ruffle. Add very dark shading along the horns, eyes, mouth, and nostrils.

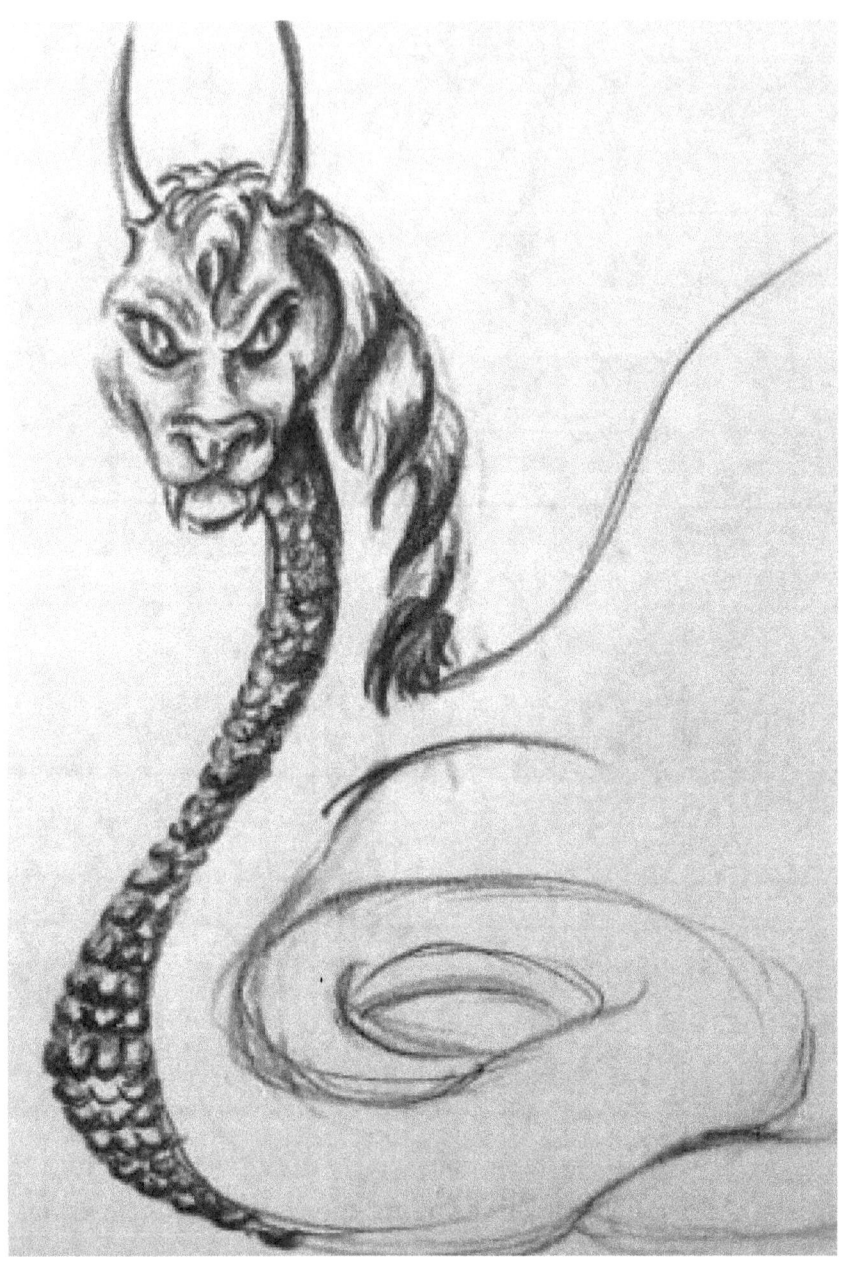

Drawing #6- Now it's time to add about three rows of scales along the belly portion of the dragon. These should be drawn fairly dark, with the darker marks being put in at the bottom of the scales.

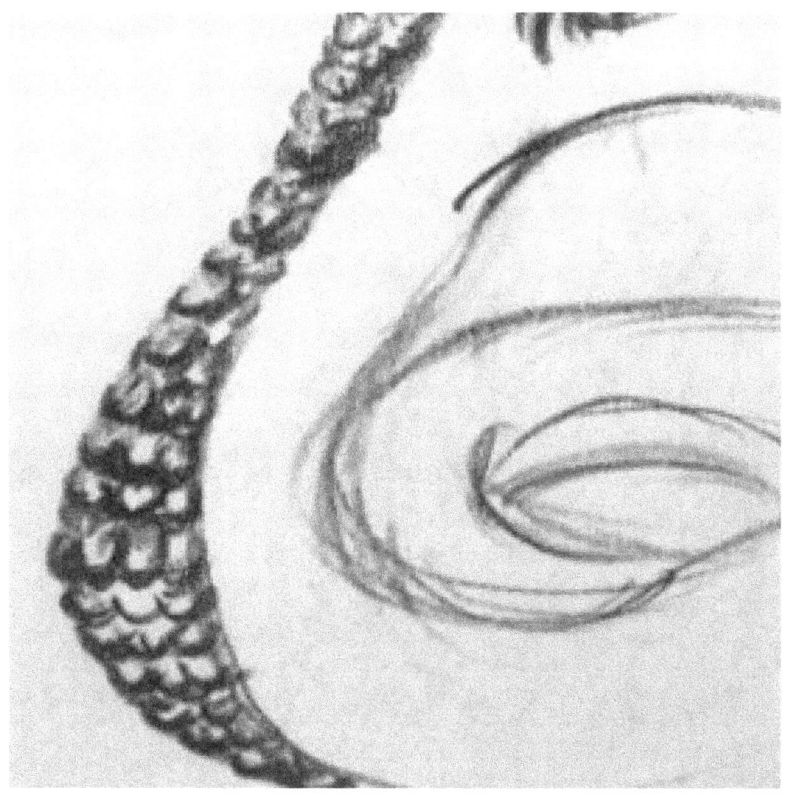

Drawing #7- Here's a more close-up view of the scales on the belly, Notice there is more subtle shading added here and there above the darker portion on the curves of the scales.

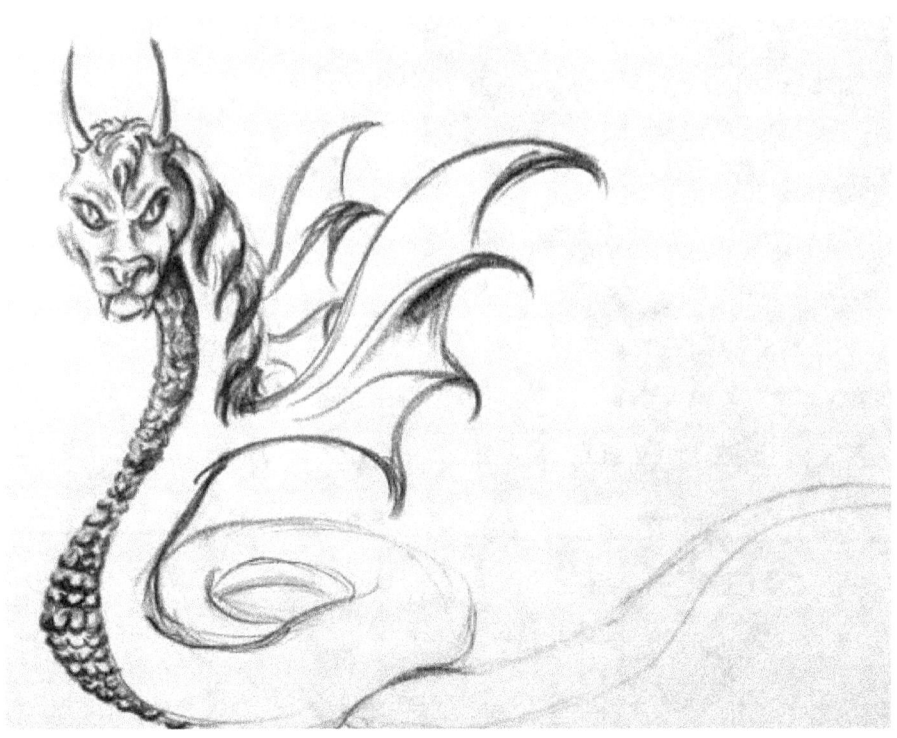

Drawing #8- Now, add the wings to your dragon. The right wing should have four curvy points at the end of the wings. Give your second point on the right wing some shading that extends into the middle; and give each point some darker shading along the bottom. The left wing will only have three points with the third one being hidden from view.

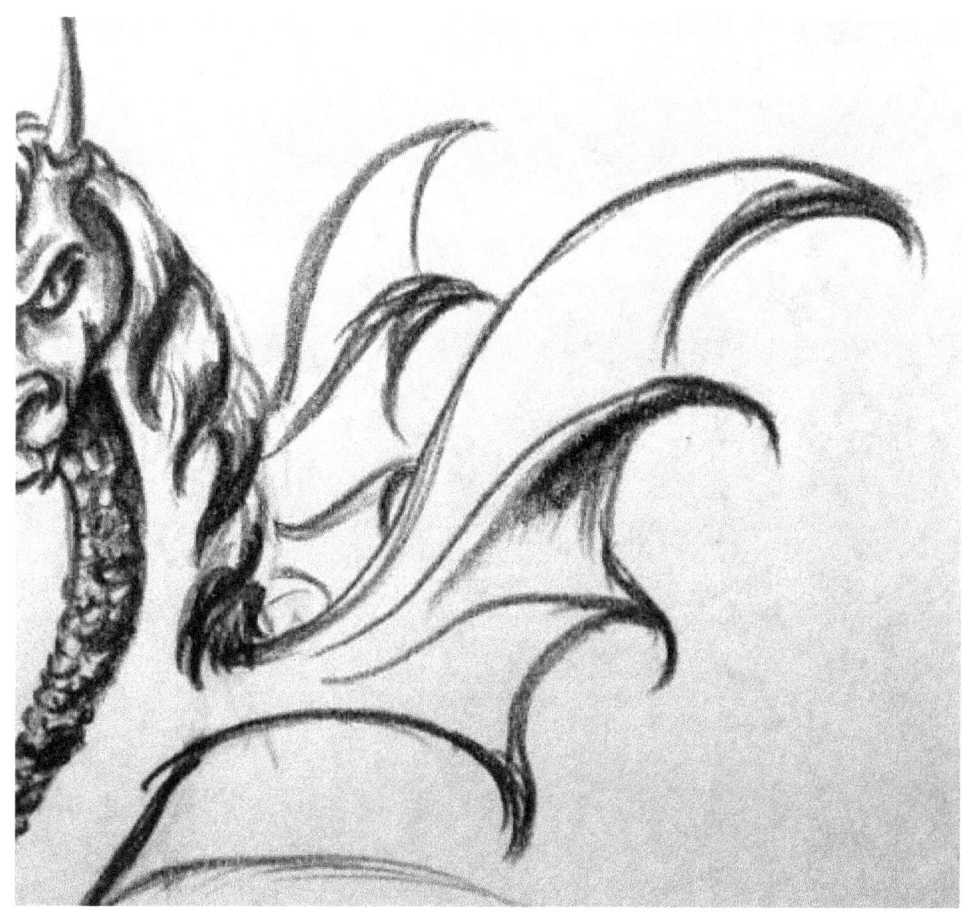

Drawing # 9- This is a close-up view of the wings. Again, notice the darker

shading along the bottom edge of the wing tips.

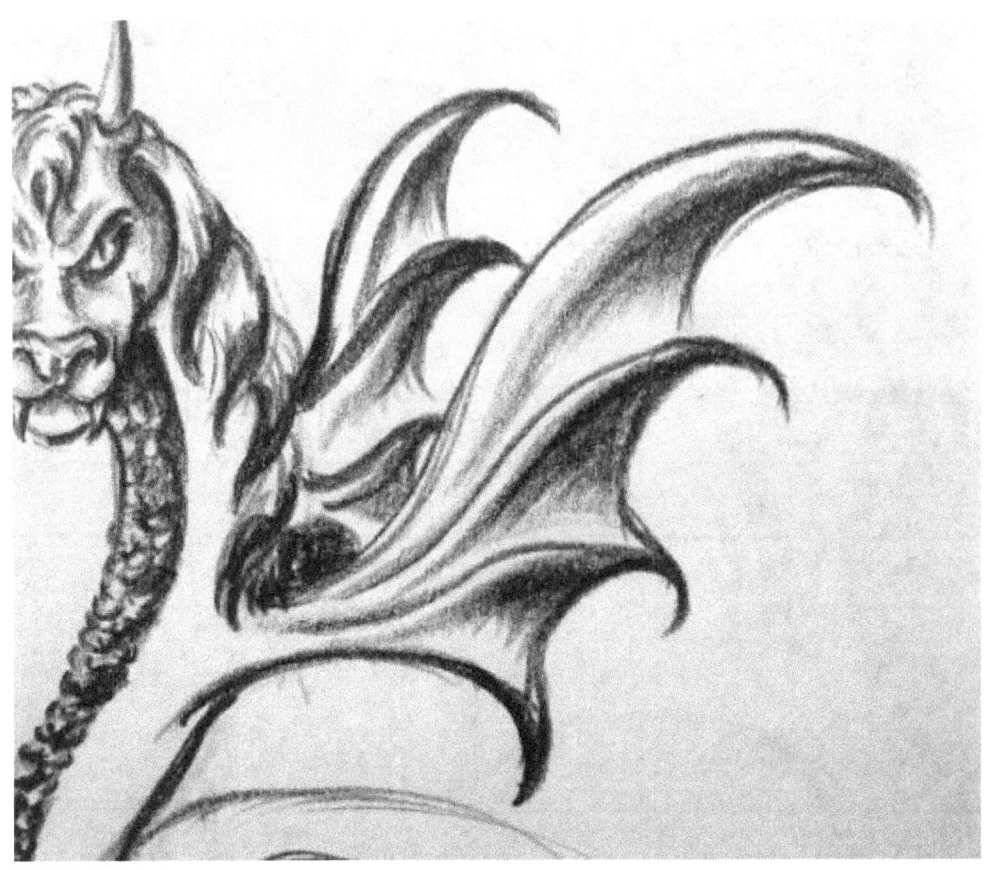

Drawing #10- On each curved portion of the wings add more shading that extends into each point from the edge. The shading should be fairly dark; but lighter as the shading extends towards the bottom of each curve of the wing.

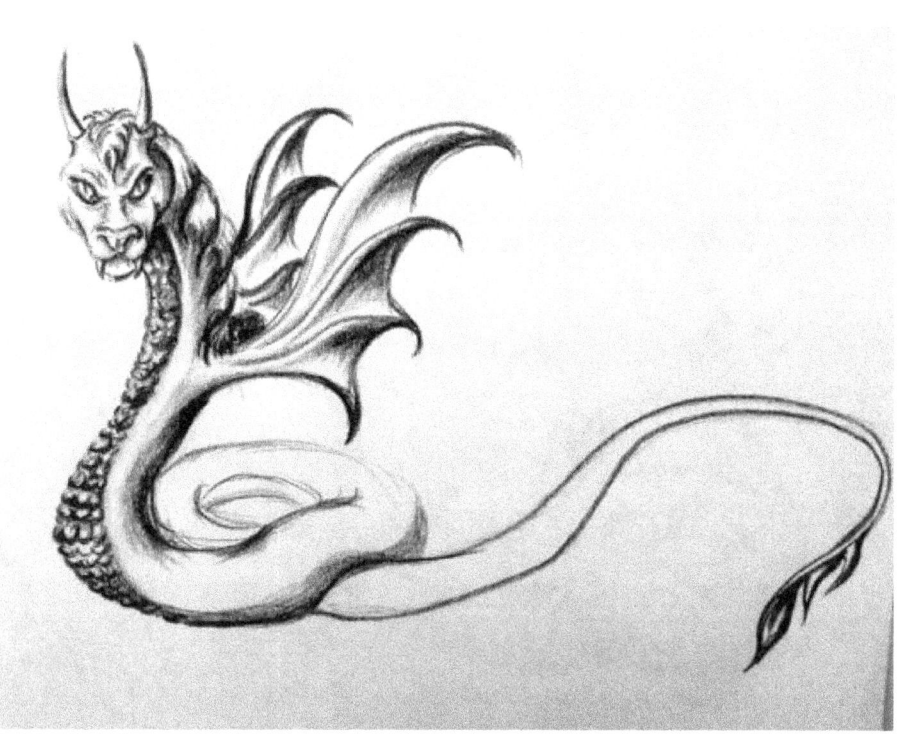

Drawing #11- Now, draw over the dragon's snake-like body with darker marks; add some darker shading along the right edge of the snake-like body. Add three tail spikes with darker shaded marks along the edges.

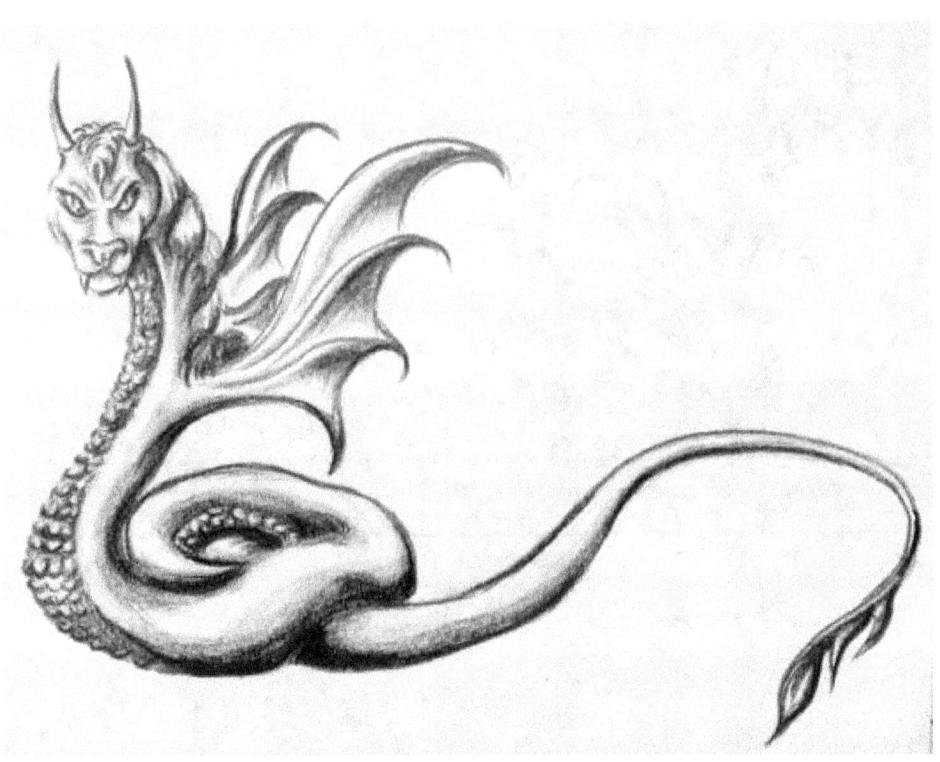

Drawing #12- Add some belly scales to the coiled portion of the dragon's tail and more dark shading along the bottom of the snake-like body. Put in some lighter, more-subtle shading that extends up from the darker shaded portions of the body and tail. Now you've completed your dragon!

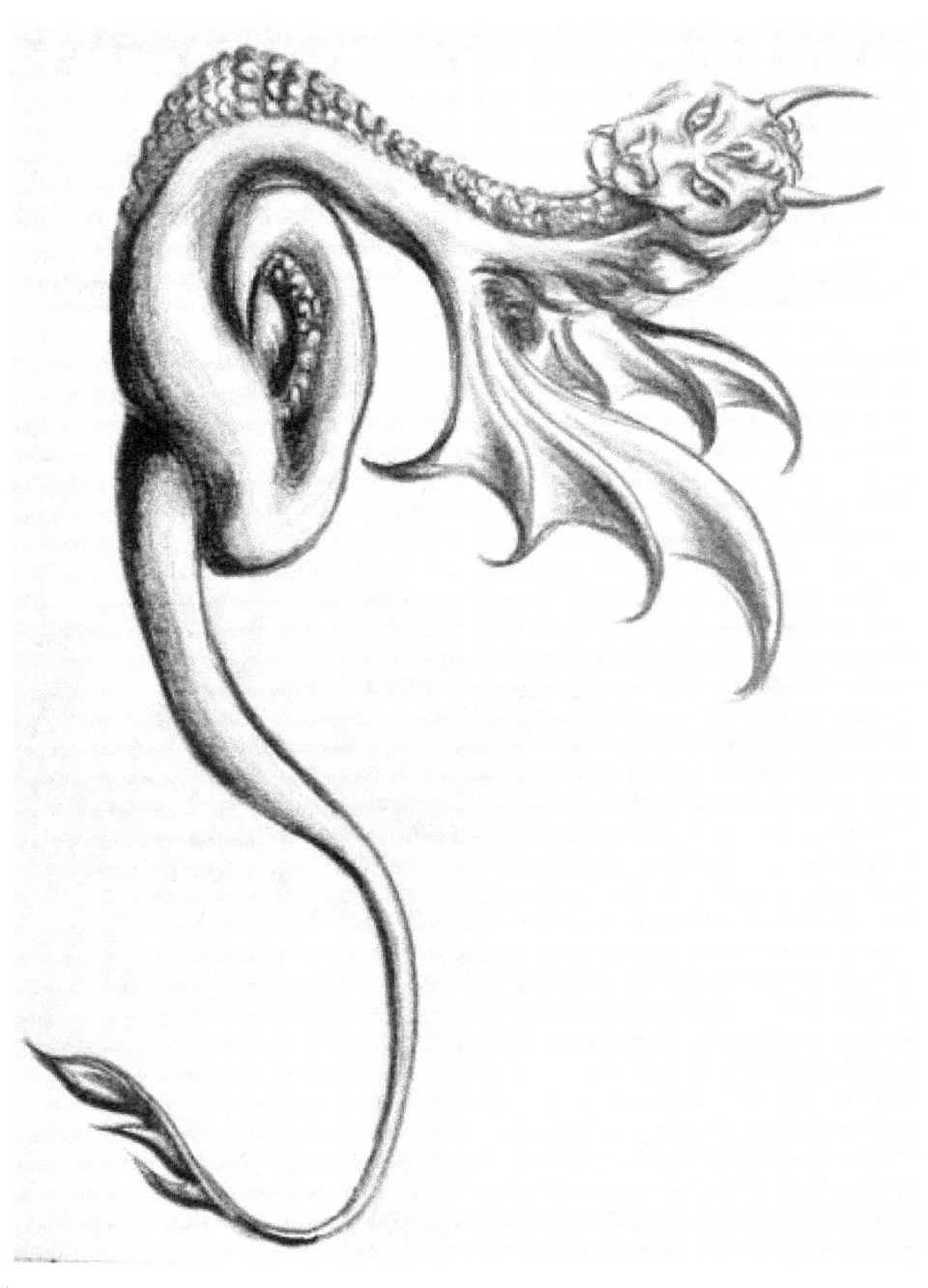

Chapter 3 – Dragon with wings spread

Here is a magnificent beast with its wings spread as if it might take flight at any moment. This dragon is a depiction quite similar to dragons as they are depicted in the European tradition. This dragon is unique because many dragons depict the front limbs as being part of the wings. This one shows a dragon with four limbs in addition to the two wings.

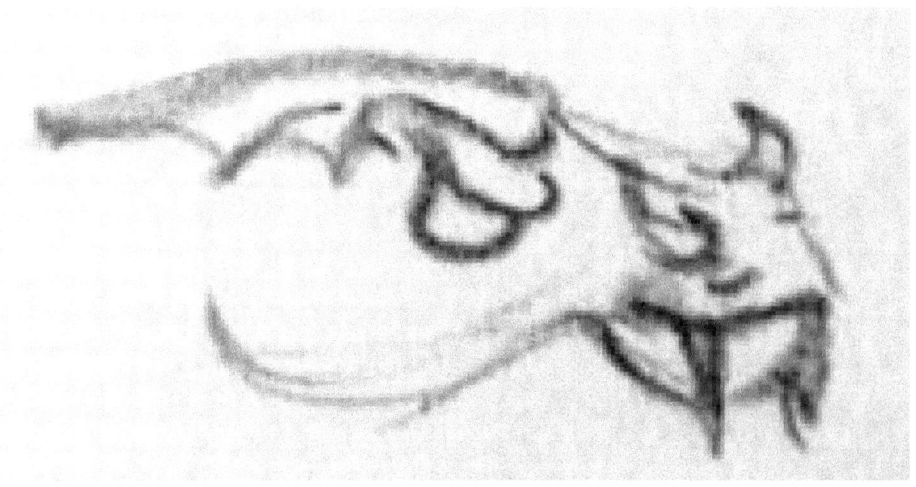

Drawing #1- Make a 'peanut' shape with your pencil that will be the shape of the dragon's head. Add the eye, mouth and two fangs. Put two horns and a small mark for its nostrils. Use a little light shading to create the small folded wing on top of its head.

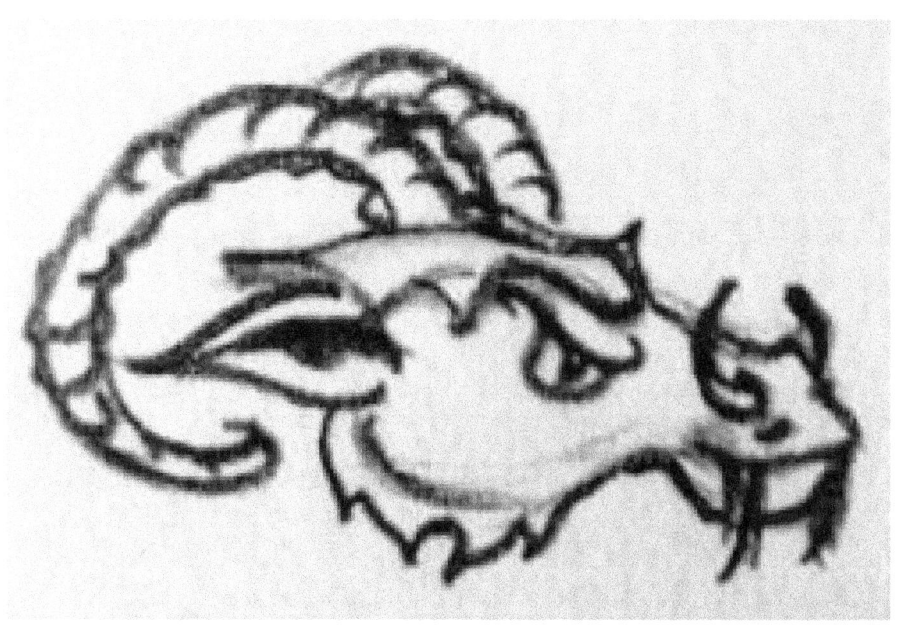

Drawing #2-Go over the outline of the dragon's head with bold strokes. Add an ear with dark shading in the center. Draw in two curved antlers with banded marks. Put in three or four neck ruffles. Make all of these marks bold and dark.

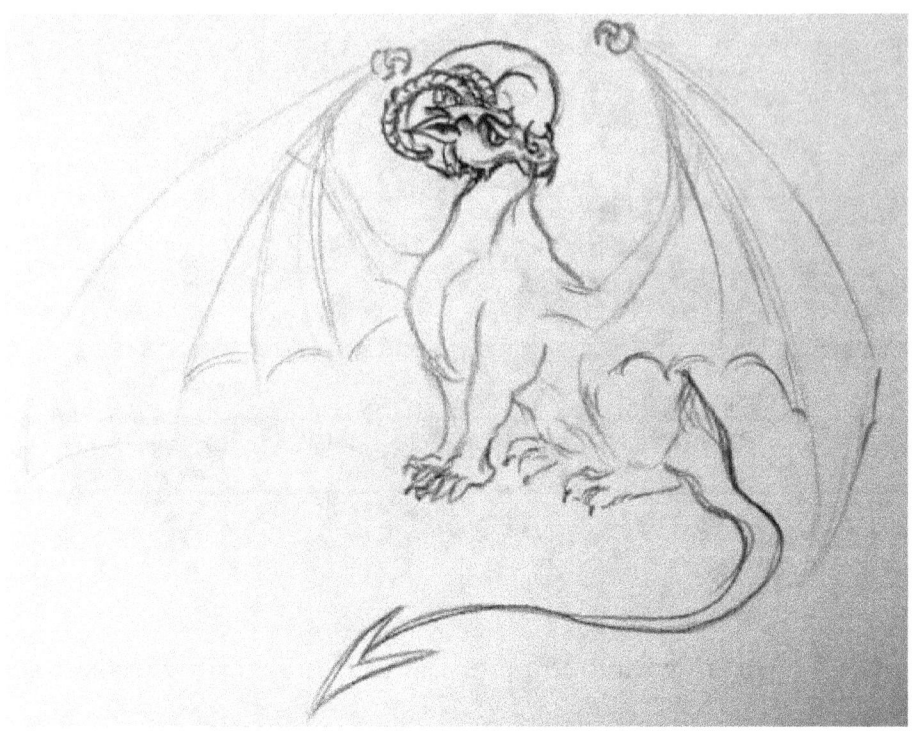

Drawing #3-From the head you drew draw in a curved neck and lightly sketch the body of the dragon with a long, pointed tail. Add two wings that are spread out with talons on the end. Add some light shading as indicated in the drawing around the eye and up to the nostril.

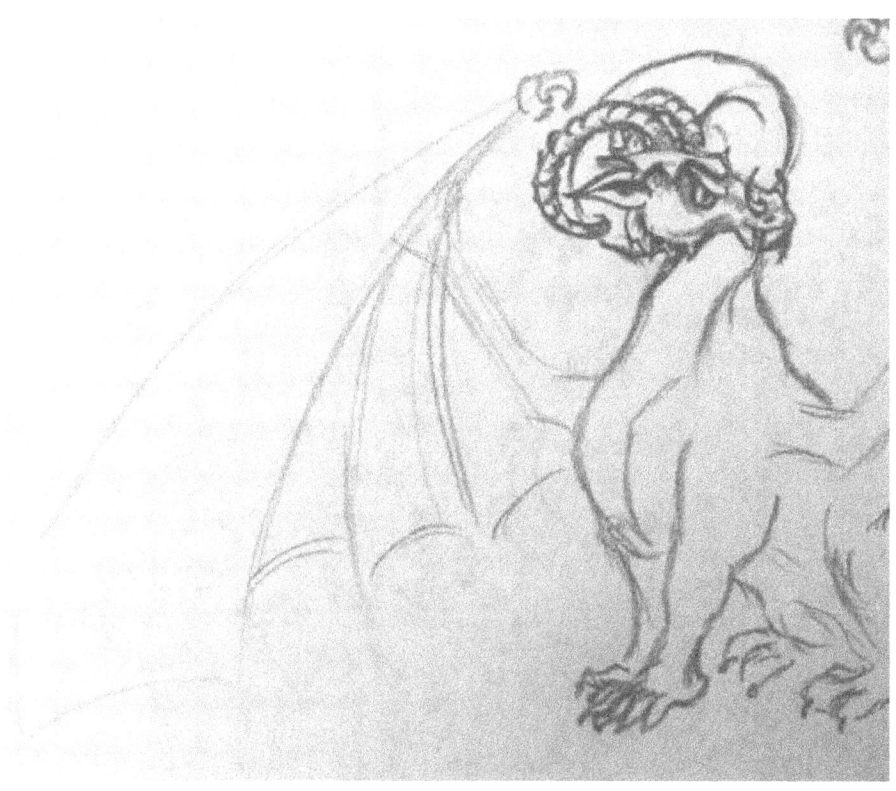

Drawing #6-Make darker, bolder strokes over the outline of the dragon's body.

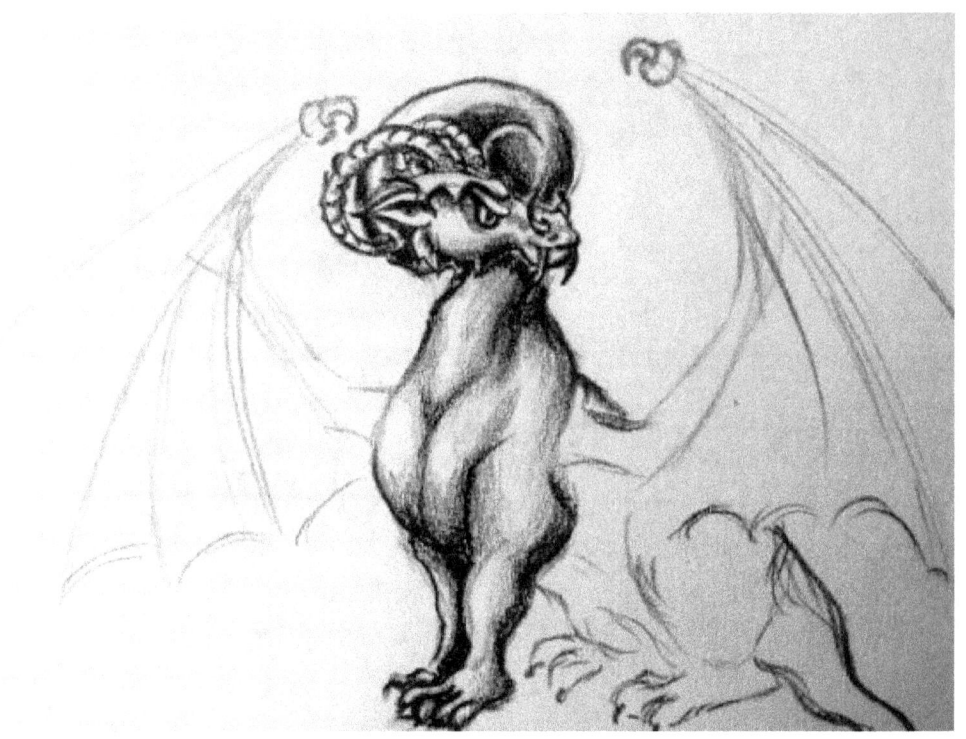

Drawing #9- Add some darker shading in between the legs and along the edges of the legs and neck. Draw in some lighter shading that extends from the darker regions on the legs, belly, neck, and head.

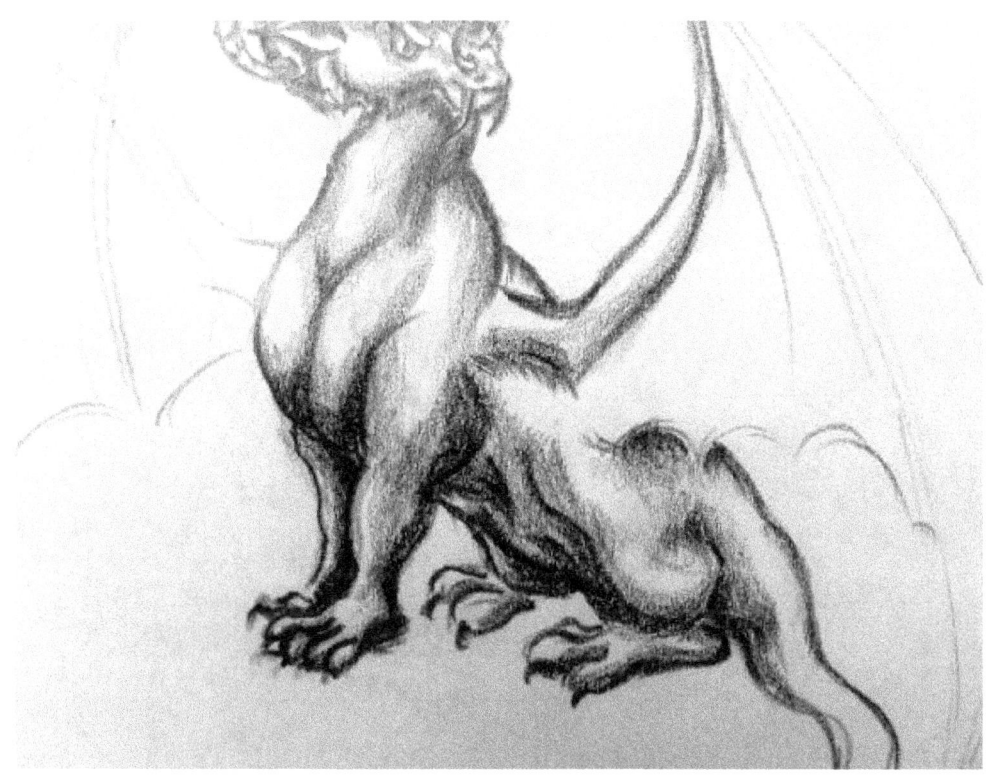

Drawing#11- Add darker shading to the hind legs and top portion of the tail. Then, draw in lighter shading that extends up from the darker regions.

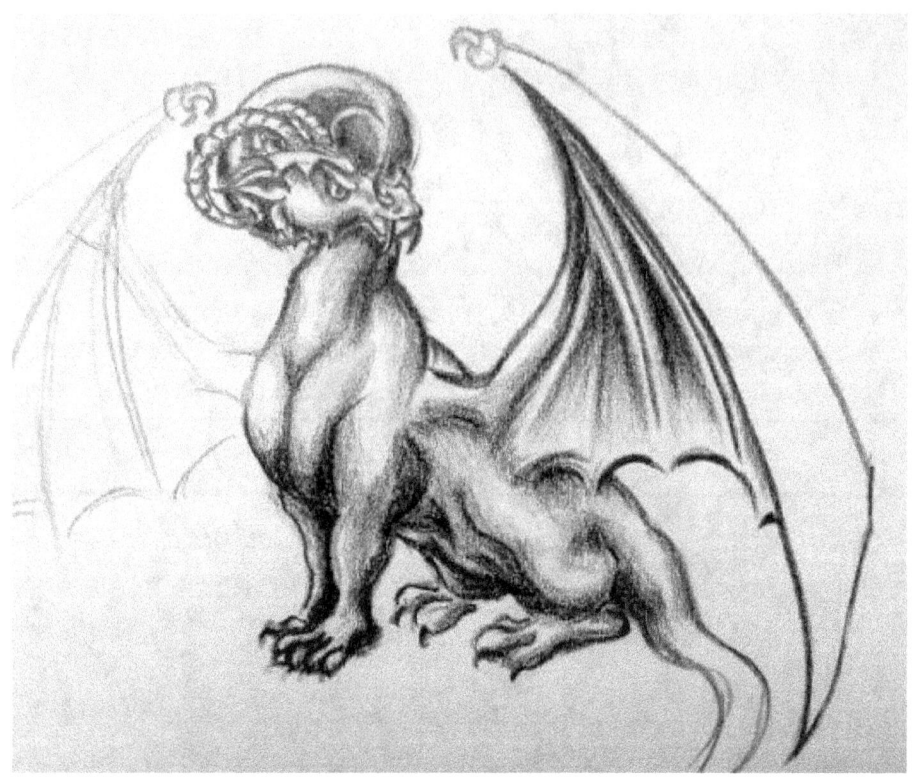

Drawing #13- Draw in five dark lines on the right wing. Leave some white areas around some of the lines as indicated in the drawing. Add some darker shading that becomes lighter as it extends from the lines in a triangular pattern as shown in the drawing. Add some darker marks along the bottom of the wing.

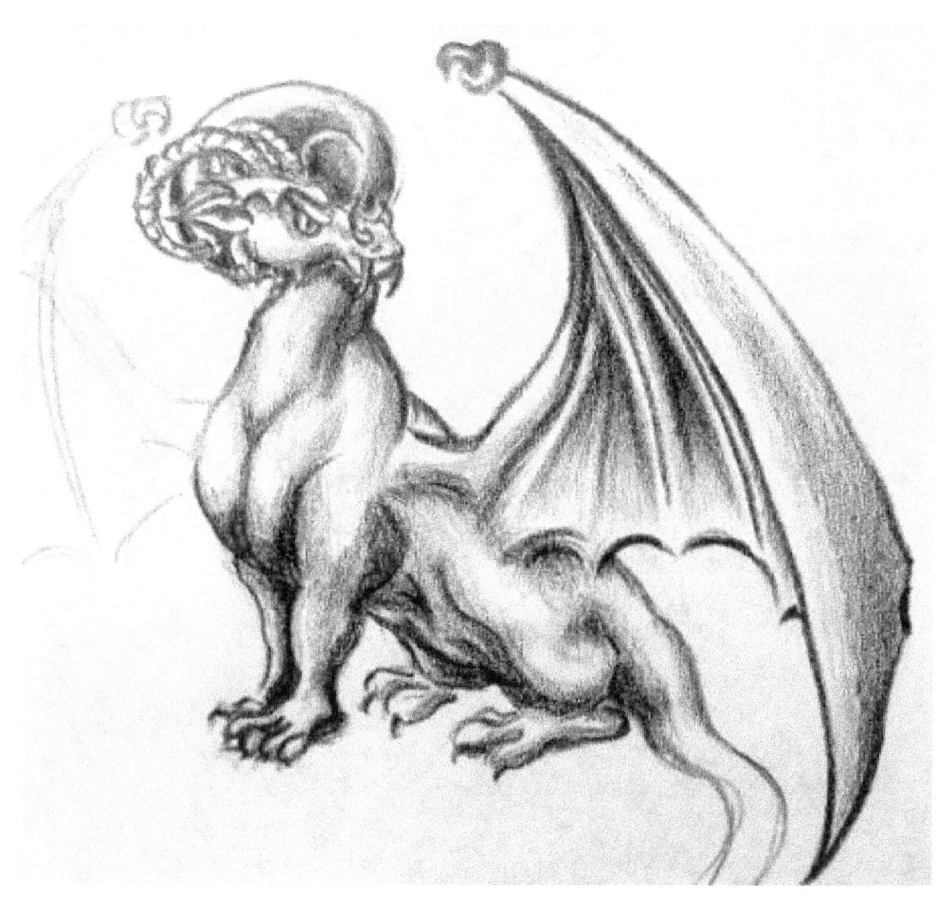

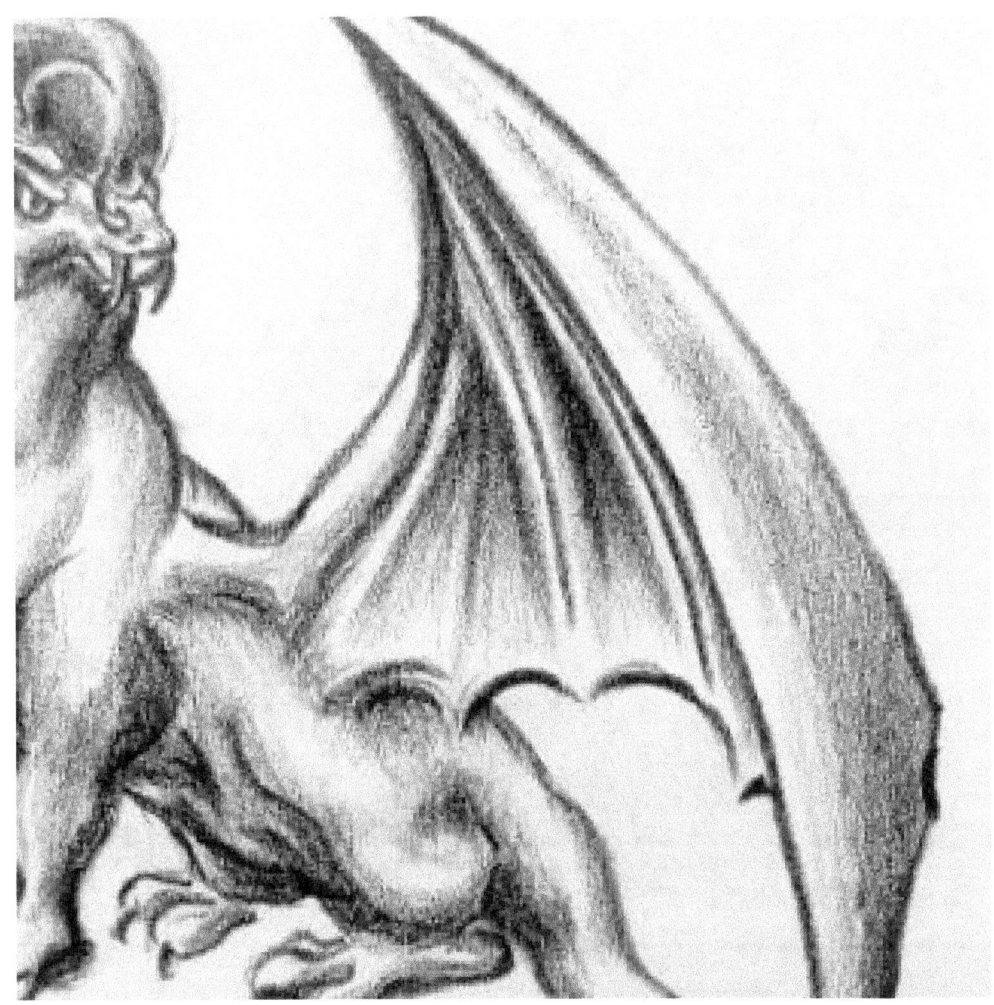

Drawing #15- Add some light shading along the right side of the outer portion of the right wing. Leave some white regions on the upper right portion and left portion of the outer wing.

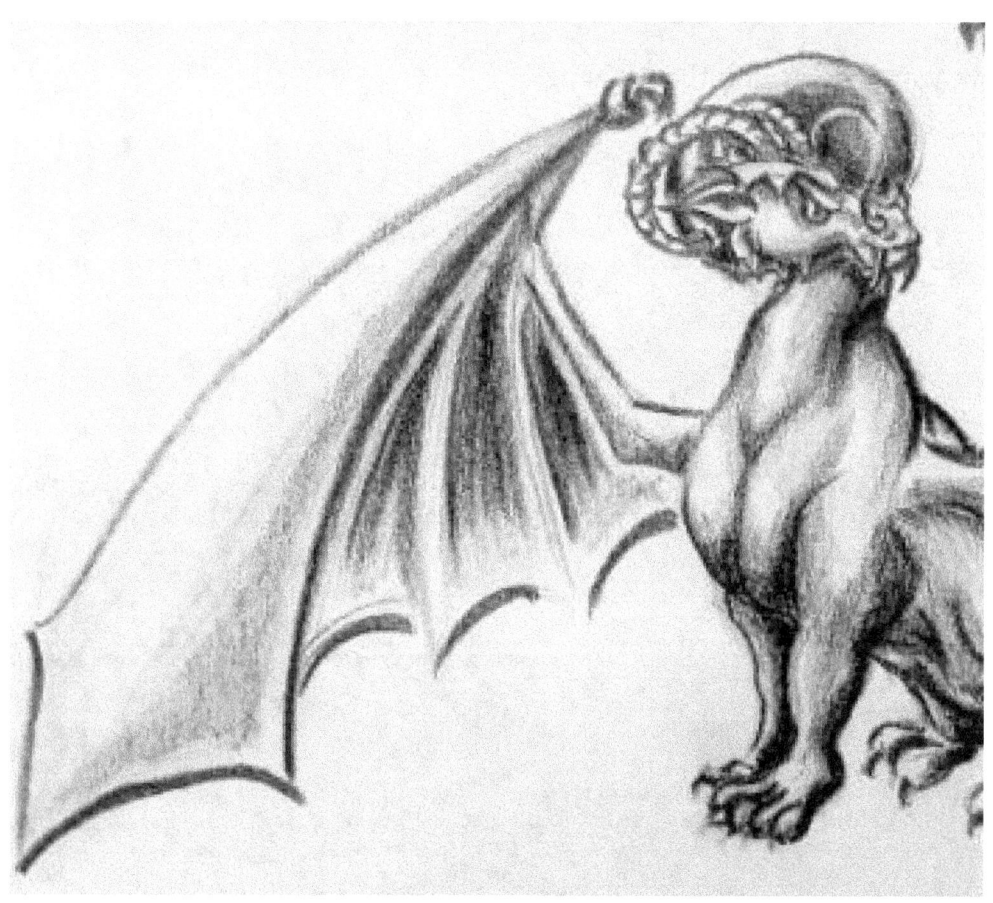

Drawing #16- Add shading to the four divided regions of the left wing in a triangular shape, just as you did with the right wing. The shading should be darker around the center and lighter as you move outwards.

Now, you're done with the drawing!

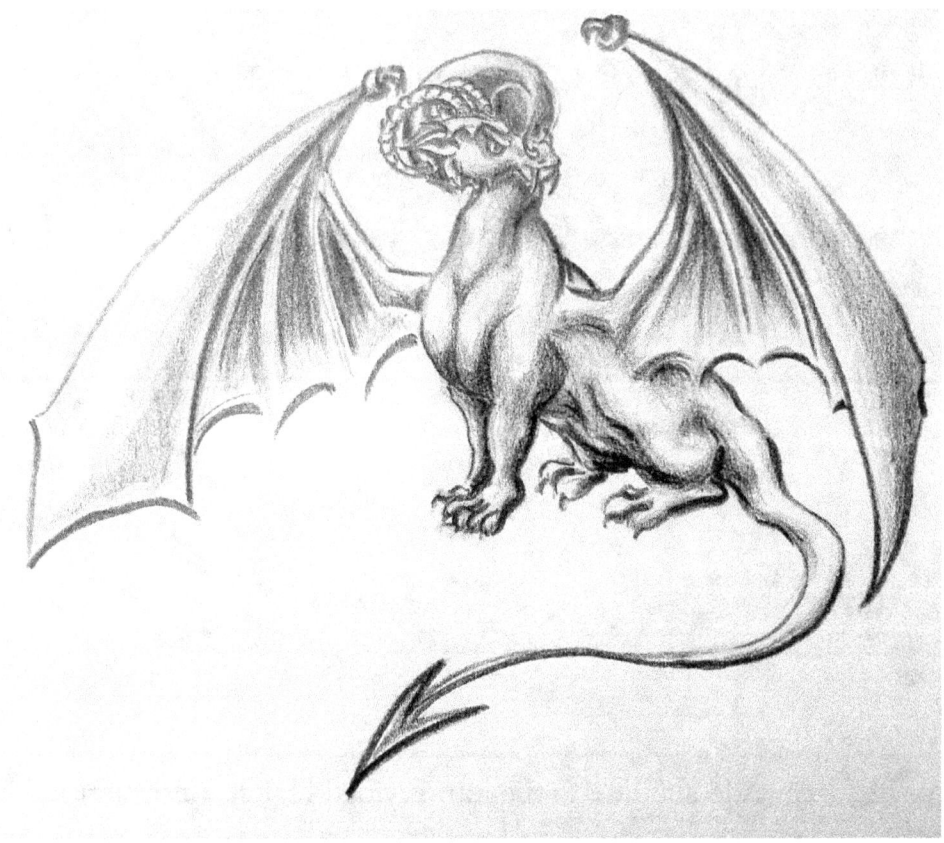

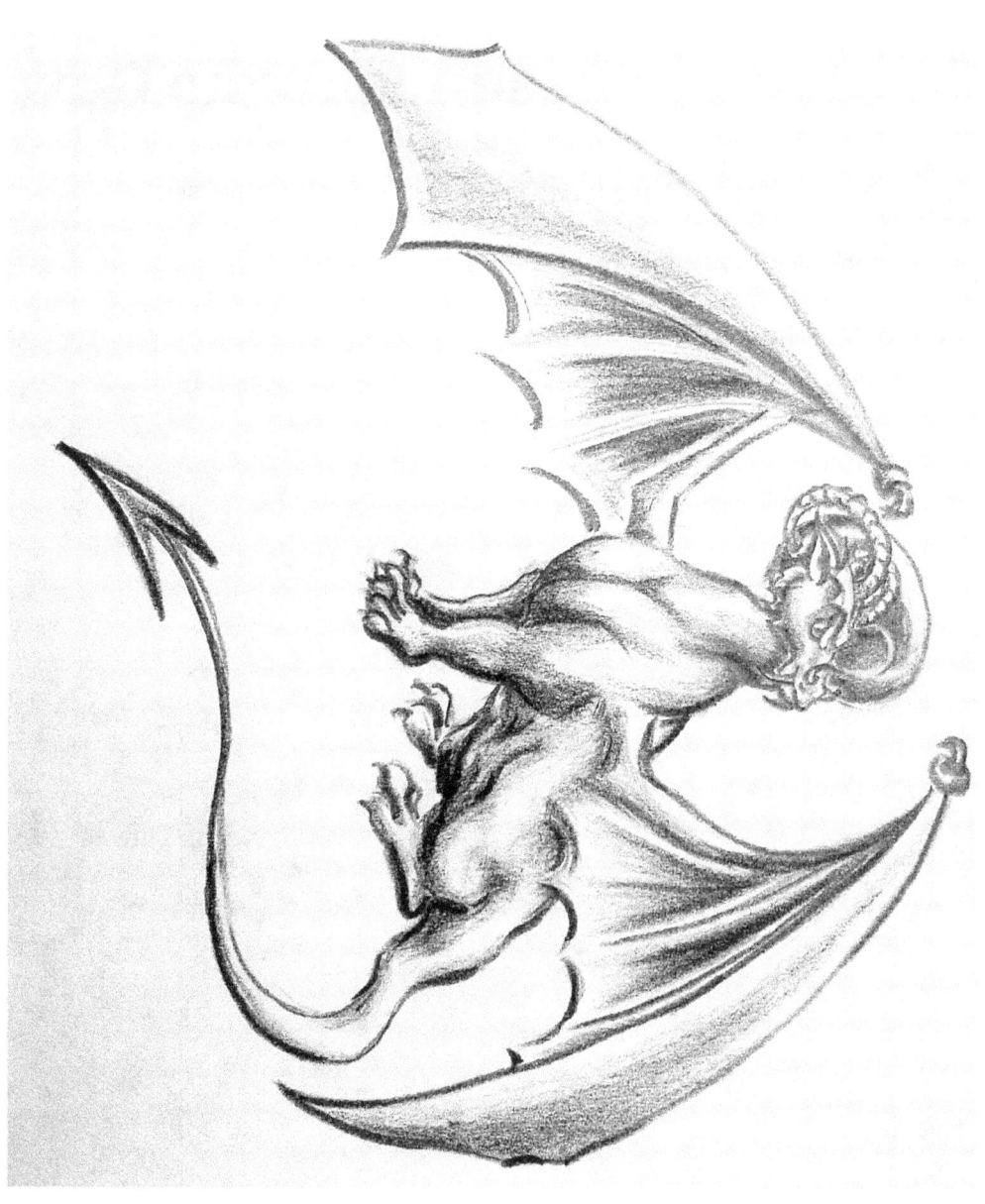

Chapter 4 – Dragonsaurus Rex

Here we have a dragon that looks a lot like a T-Rex dinosaur with classic reptilian features. This is another depiction of the European idea of the dragon with its horns and outspread wings. It looks as if it is in pursuit of it prey.

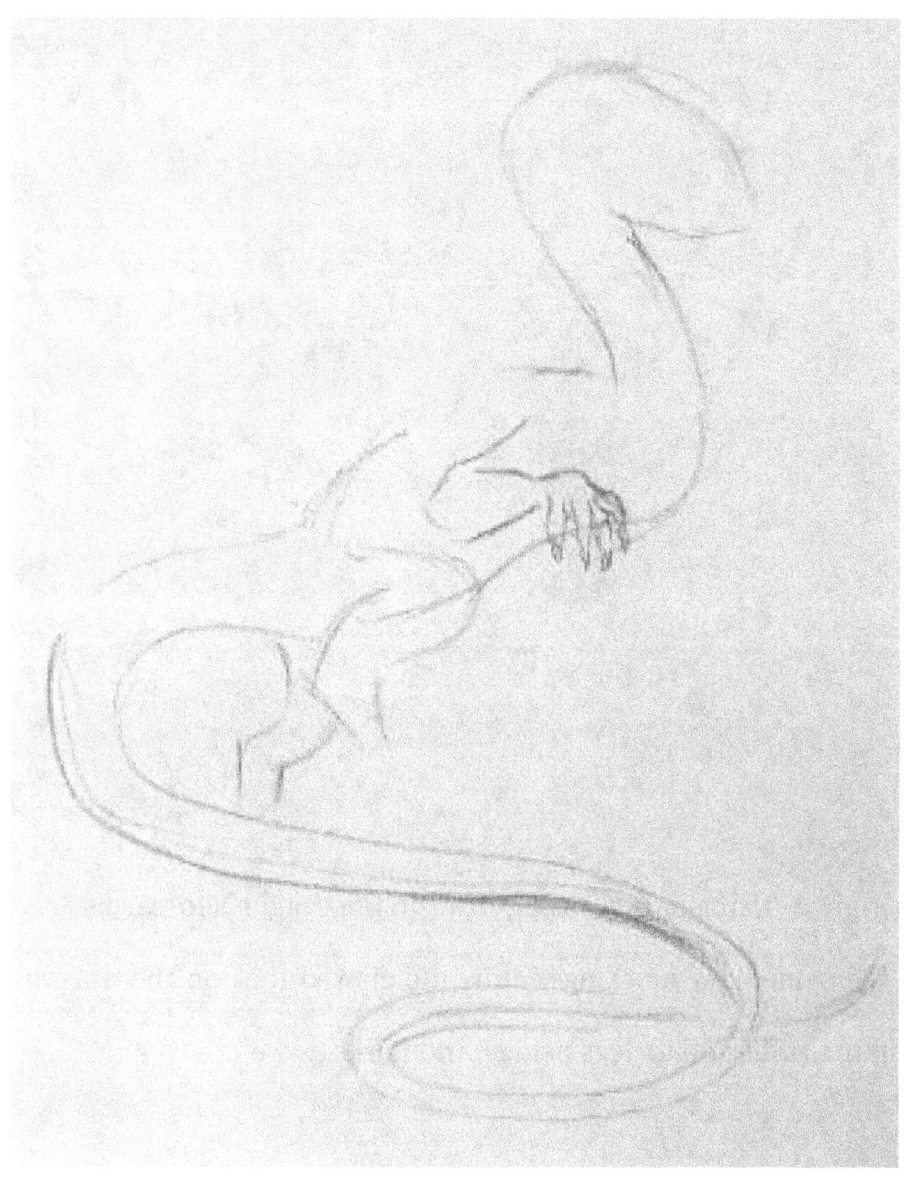

Drawing #1- Make an outline of the dragon's body with a long, curved tail.

Draw his right arm, including claws and the top part of its legs.

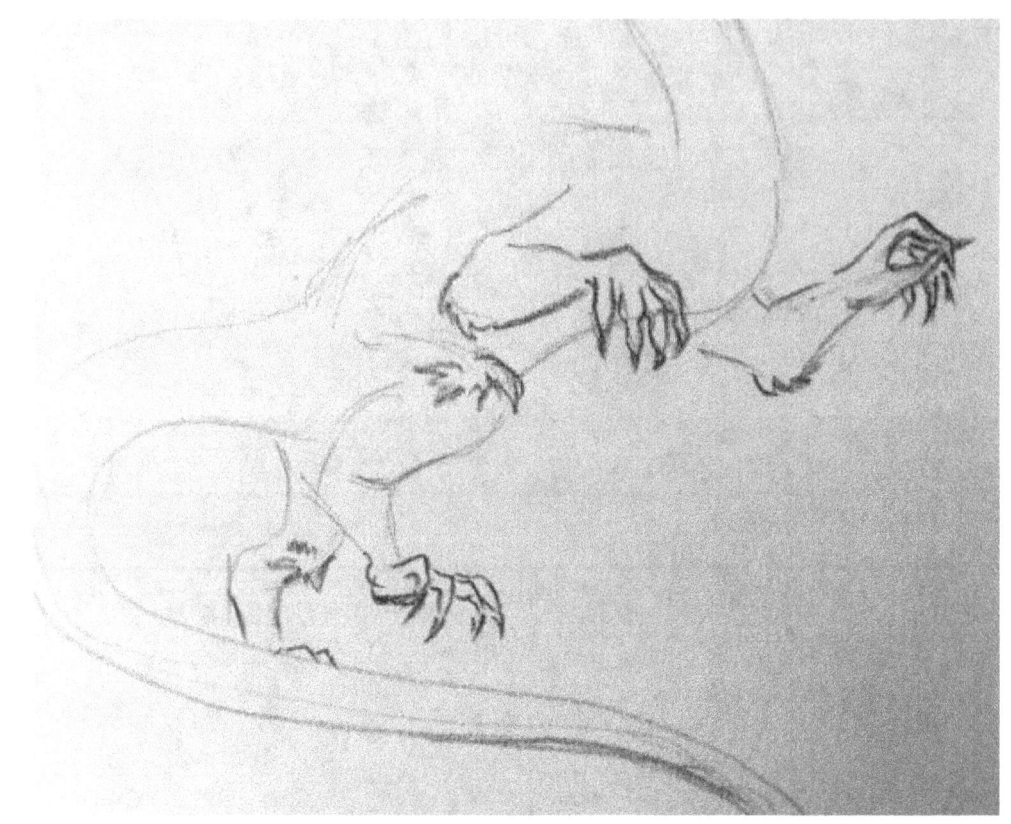

Drawing #2- Using darker marks draw in the dragon's forearms and claws.

Using the same dark markings, draw the clawed toes on the dragon's feet.

Draw in the ruffles on its legs using dark marks as well.

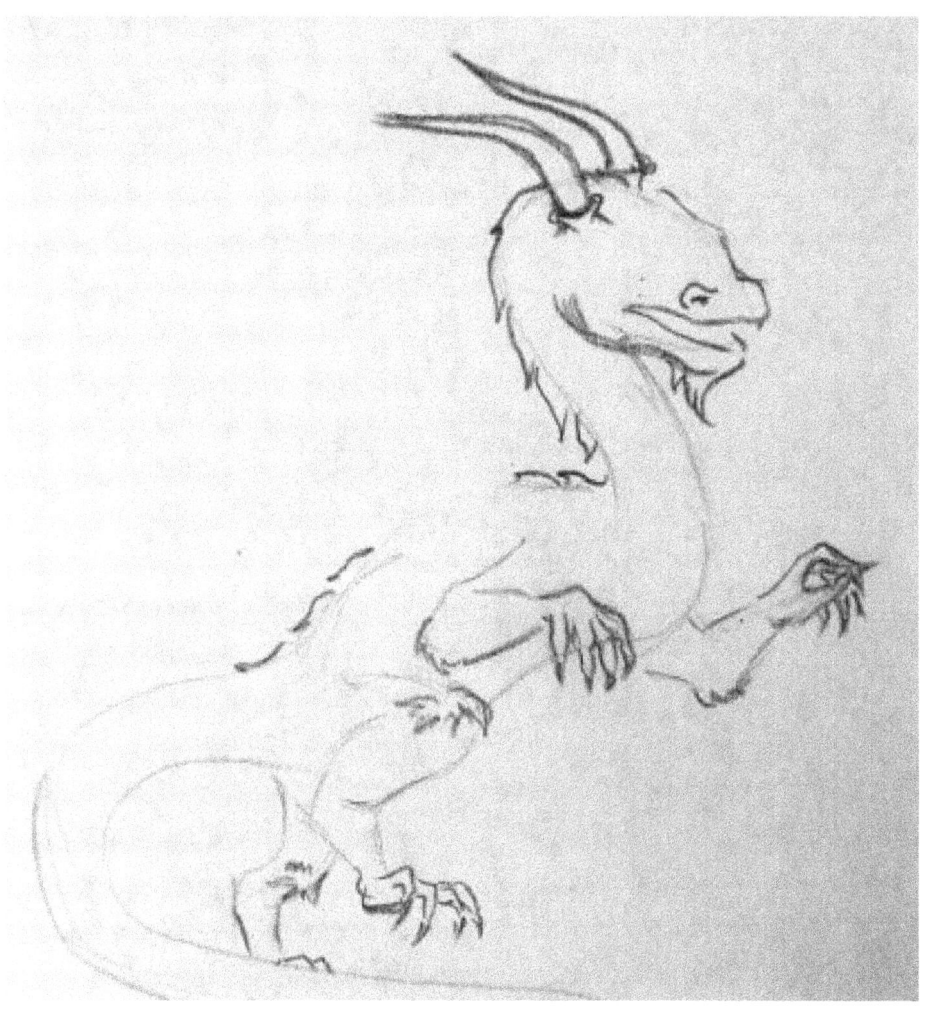

Drawing #3- Draw in the plates along the dragon's back using darker strokes. Now, draw the outline of the dragon's head and two curved horns at the top of the head. Use darker marks as you did with the claws and ruffles.

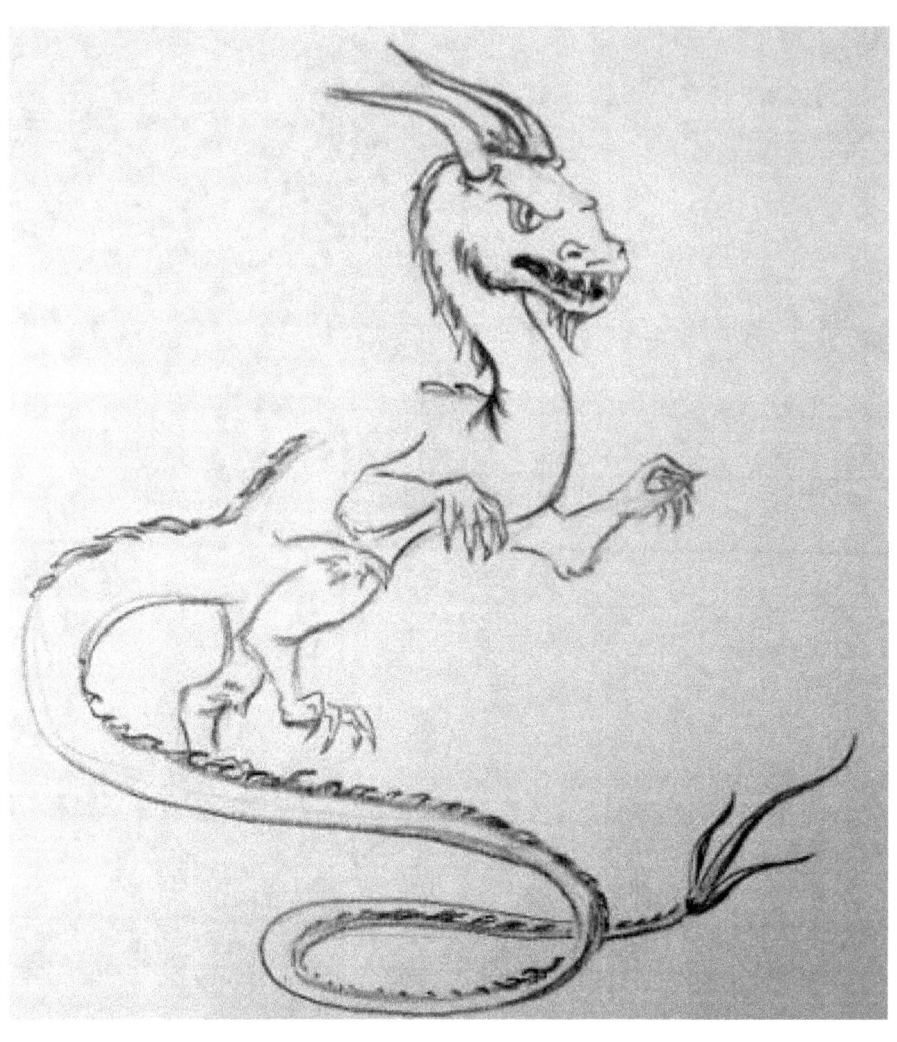

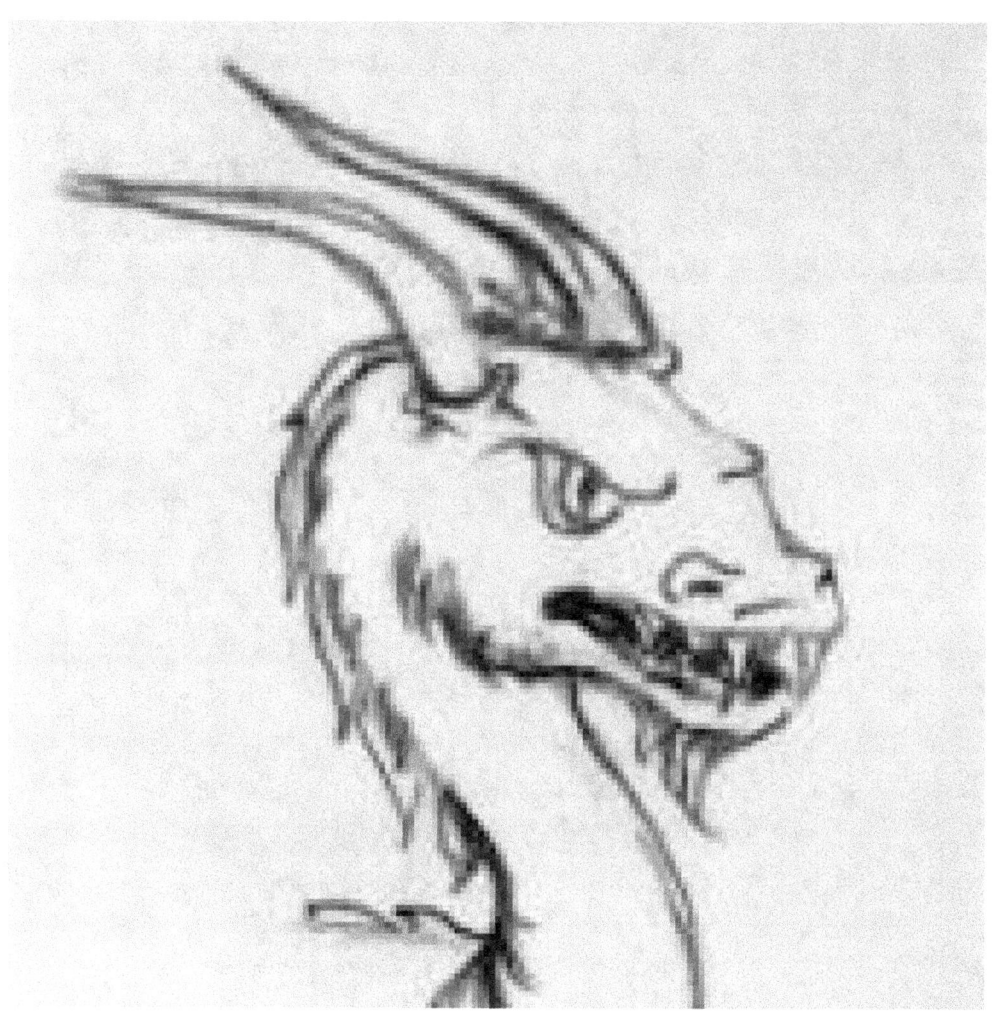

Drawing #4- Now, draw in some of the details of the dragon's face. Draw in an eye and curved teeth. Put in some dark shading inside of the mouth. Do some darker shading around the jawline and some tufts on the end of the dragon's chin. Put in some darker shading where the neck joins the body. Next, draw scaly plates where indicated on the drawing on the upper and lower portions of the tail and three long tail spikes.

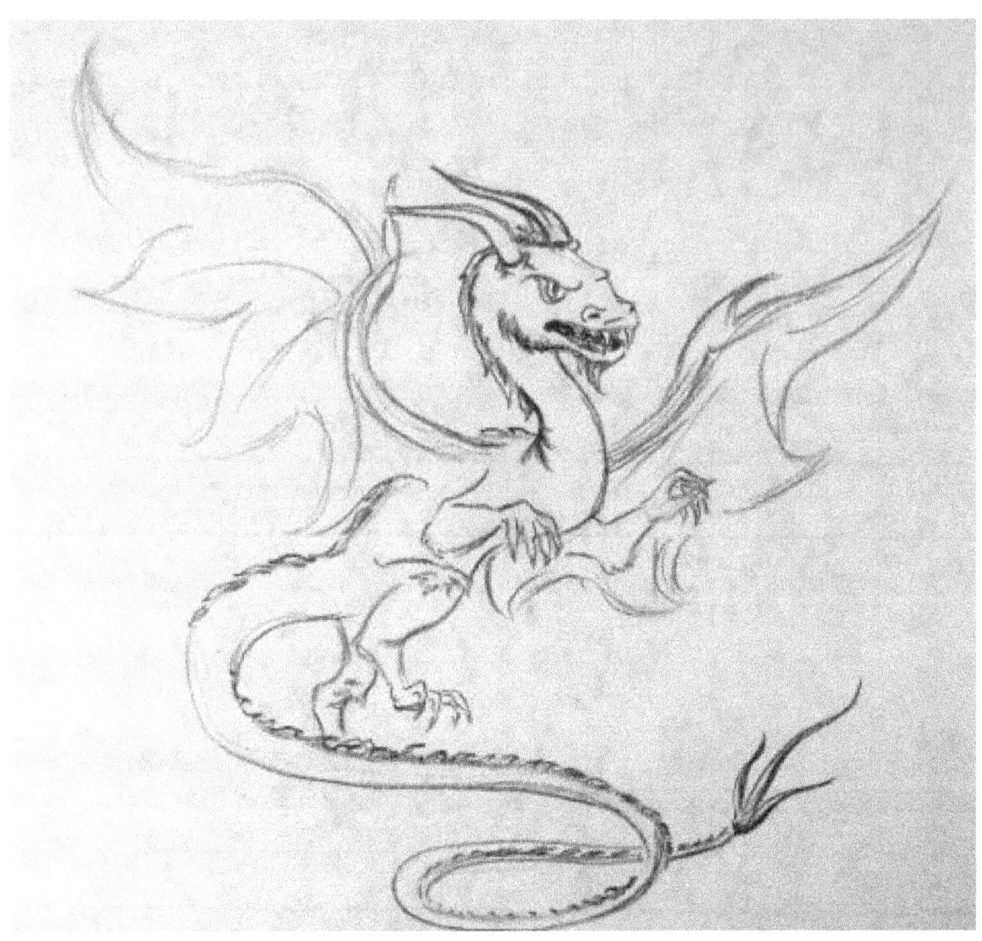

Drawing #5- It's time to give your dragon some wings! Lightly sketch the wings including four leaf-like points on them.

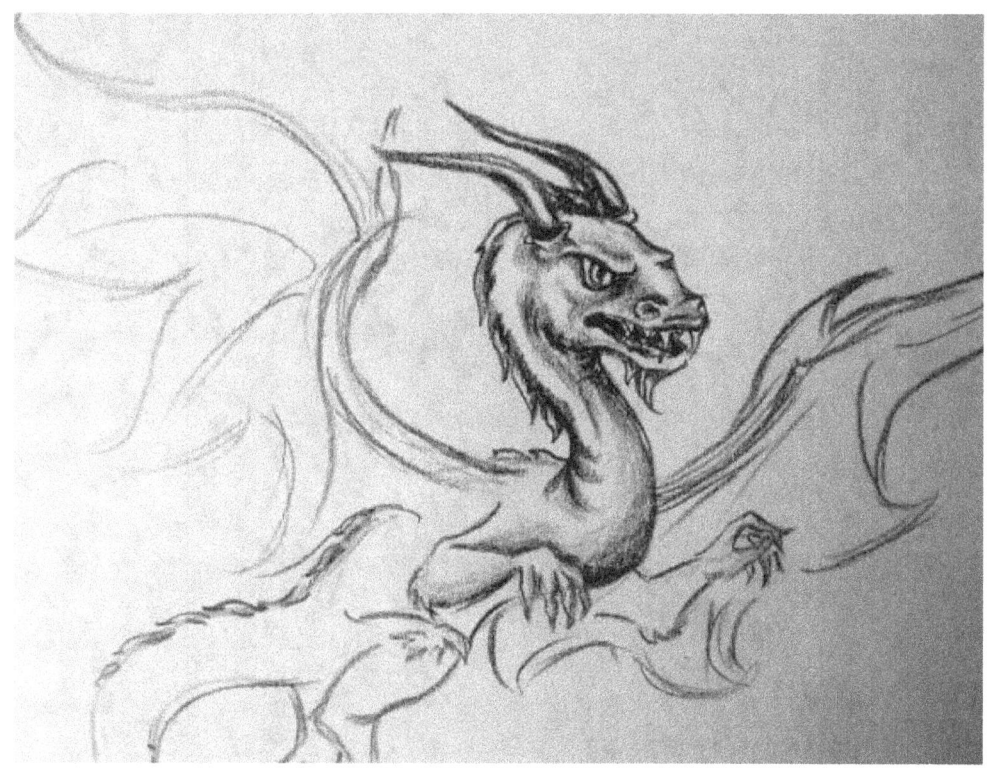

Drawing #6- Using the side of the pencil lead, add some lighter shading on the dragon's face and neck where indicated on the drawing.

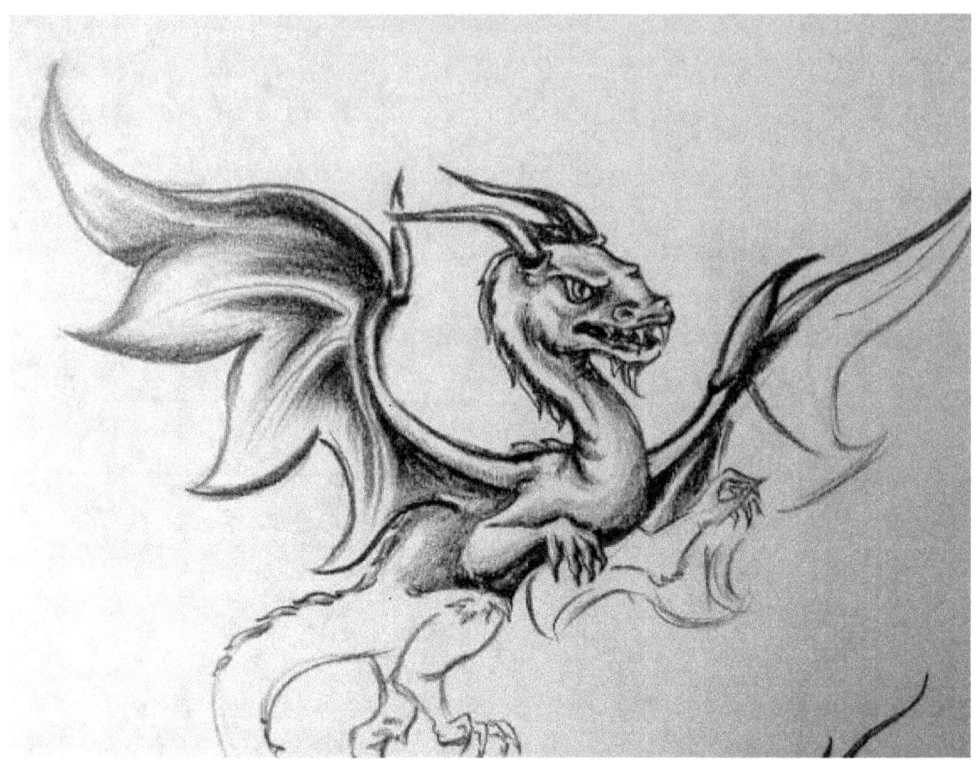

Drawing #7- Add shading to the left wing with darker shading along the top of the wings and towards the tips of the 'triangles'. Include lighter shading below the darker regions.

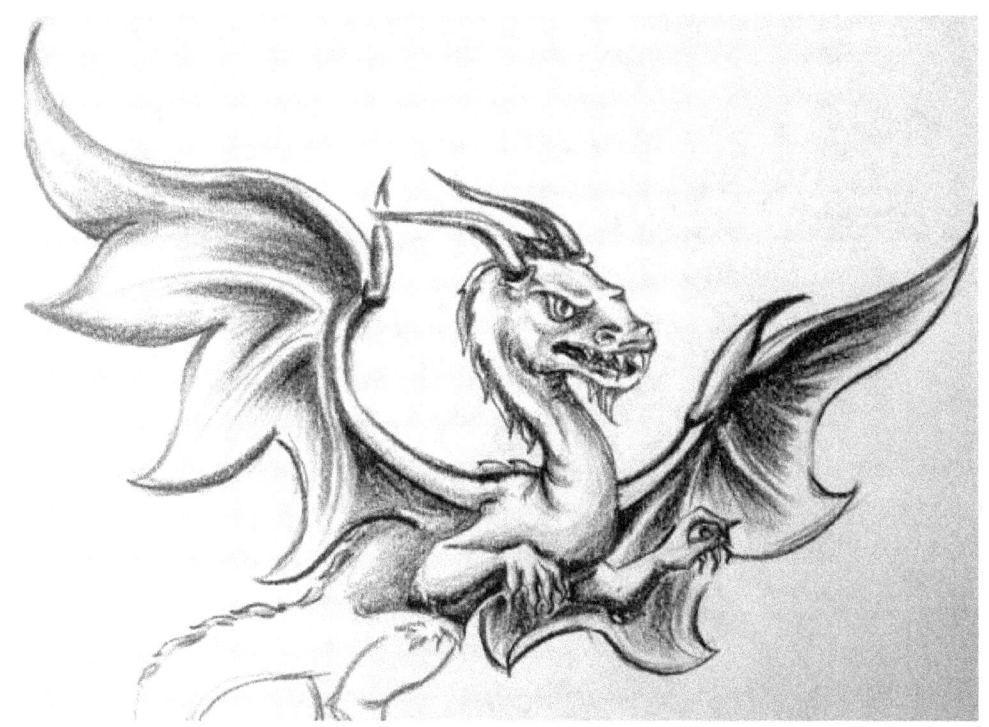

Drawing #8- Now, add shading to the right wing. Use fairly dark shading; but not as dark as the top portion of the shaded region of the wing. Also, draw in the right arm with darker marks and shading along the bottom.

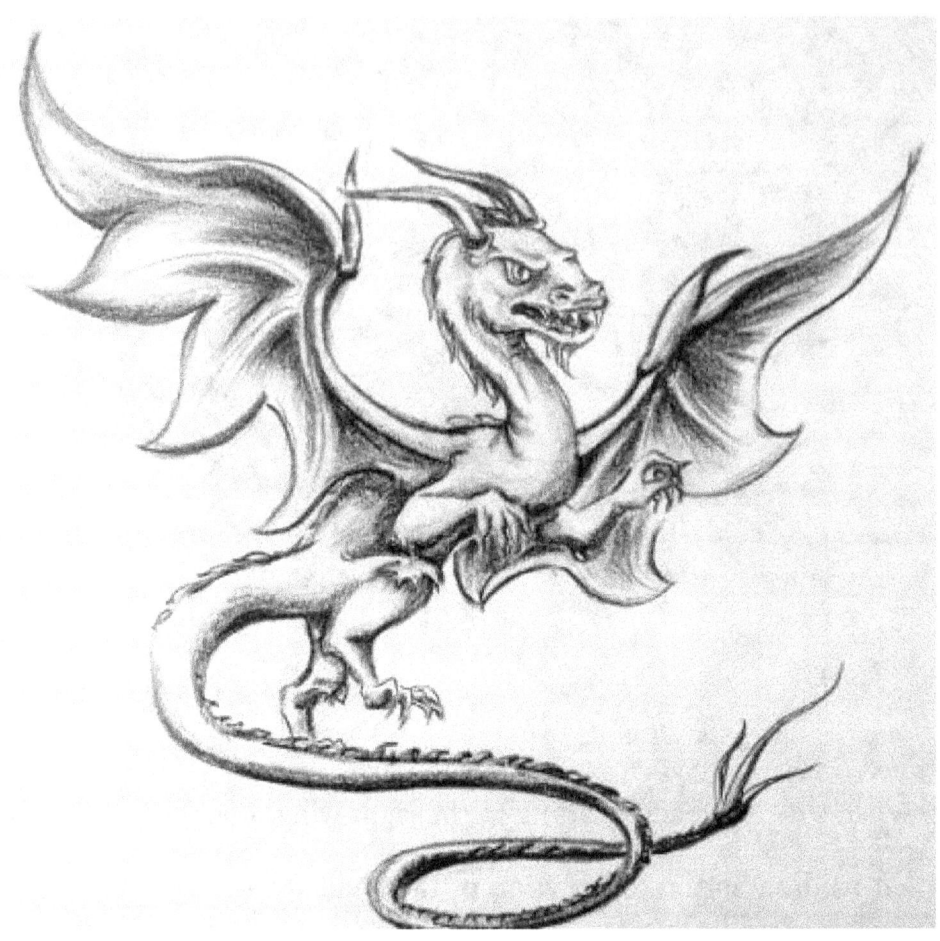

Drawing #9- Shade in the bottom portions of the tail using darker marks at the very bottom and slightly lighter shading above that. Now your dragon is complete!

Chapter 5 – Dragon on Two legs:

Here we have a formidable creature stalking its victim. As it is with the European tradition, this dragon has long, pointed scales going down its back and huge, pointed wings. One can almost picture the hero standing beside the creature in a fight to the death.

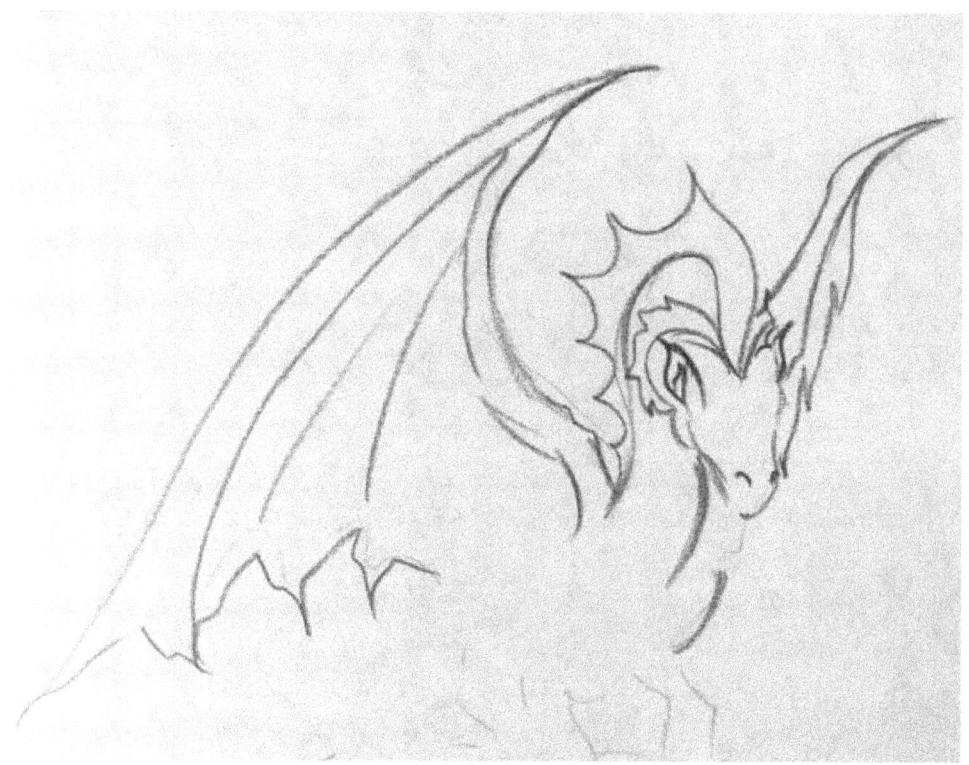

Drawing #1- Make a long, sloping line that ends in a point and curves sharply inwards. On the bottom of the left wing, make four jagged points. Add six ruffles and make the opposite wing tip. Use fairly dark marks. Make a 'v'-shaped head, two nostrils the two ears. Add some ruffles around the head. Lightly sketch the outline of the legs.

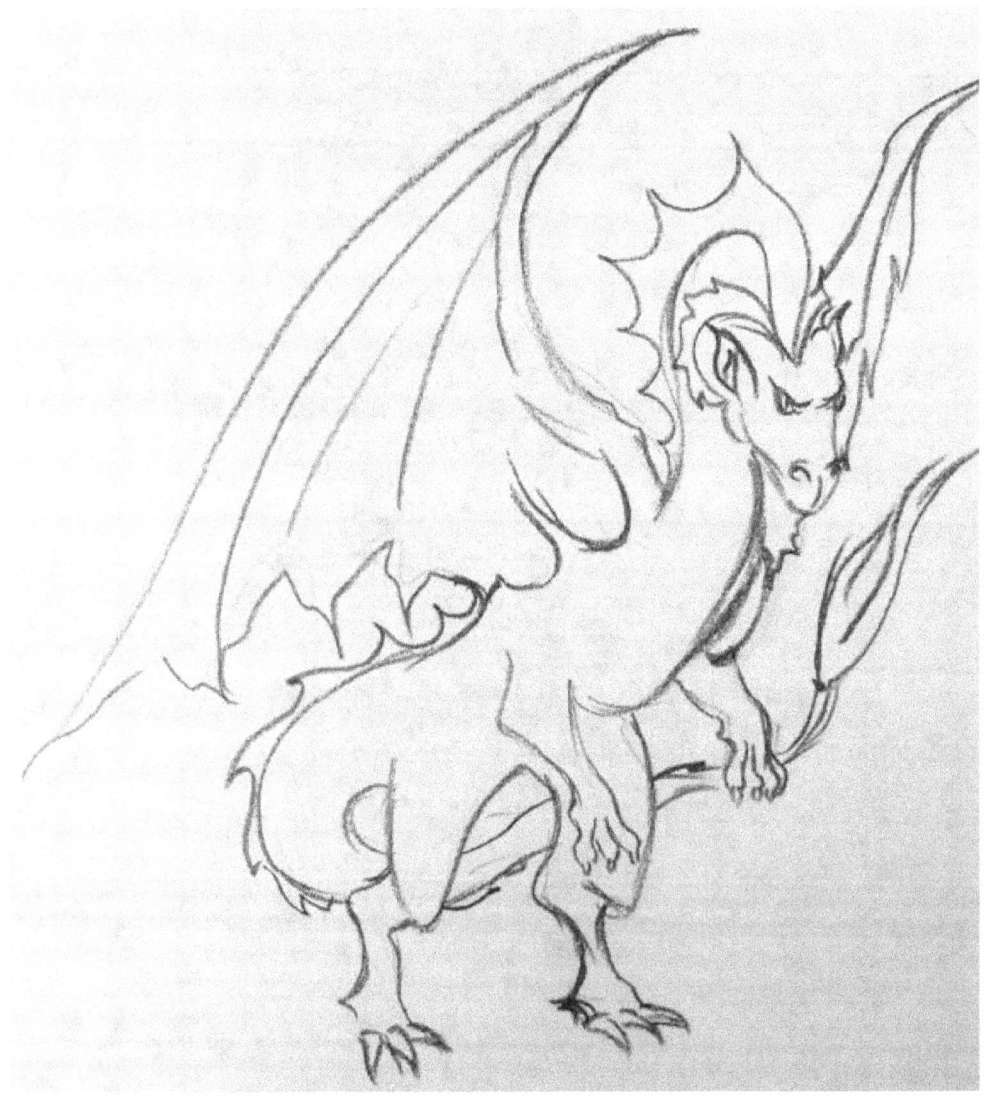

Drawing #2- From the bottom of the left wing make the curve of the tail and add spikes that line the tail. Draw two 'v'-shapes that will make up the dragon's knees. Add two legs extending from the knees with three claws on each toe. From the light sketches you made previously, add the dragon's two upper legs with three claws on each. From the left arm, draw a curved belly. Ass in the dragon's eyes and complete the nostrils form the marks you made previously. Draw in a spikey tail.

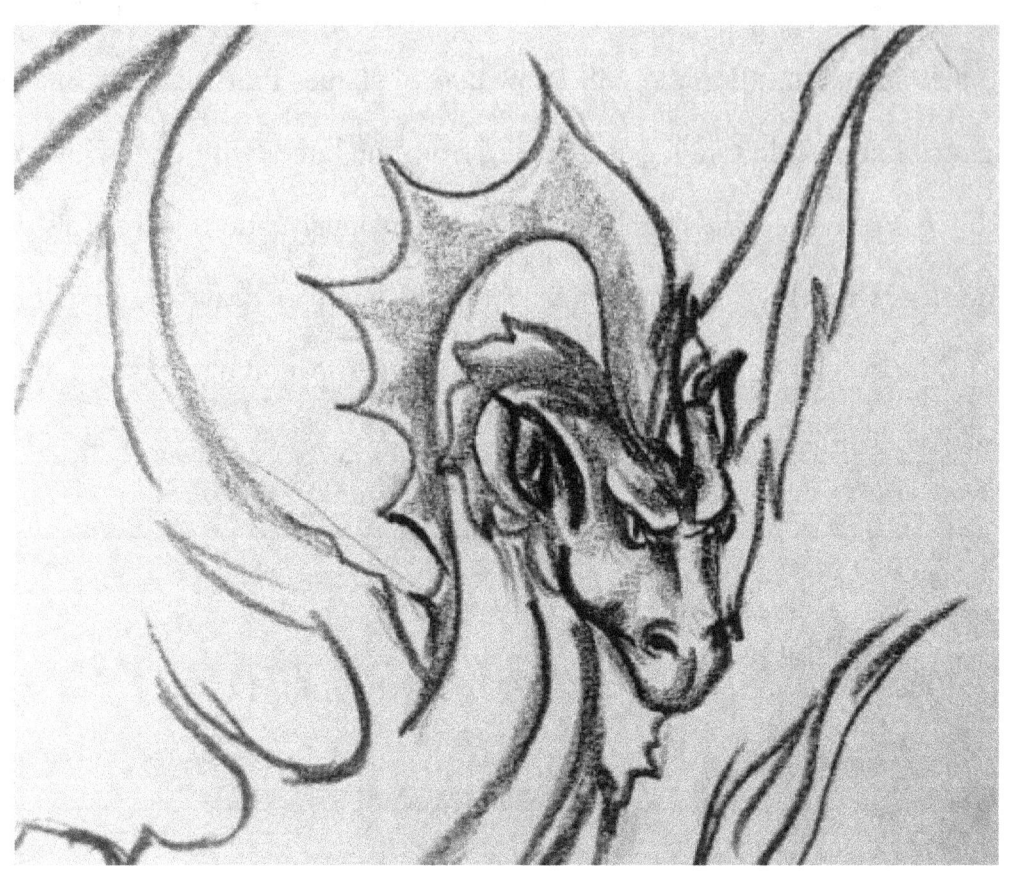

Drawing #3- Go over the outline of the dragon with thicker, darker marks. Using the side of the pencil, add triangular-shaped, shaded regions on the dragon's neck ruffles. Add in shaded regions to the face and the ruffles that surround it.

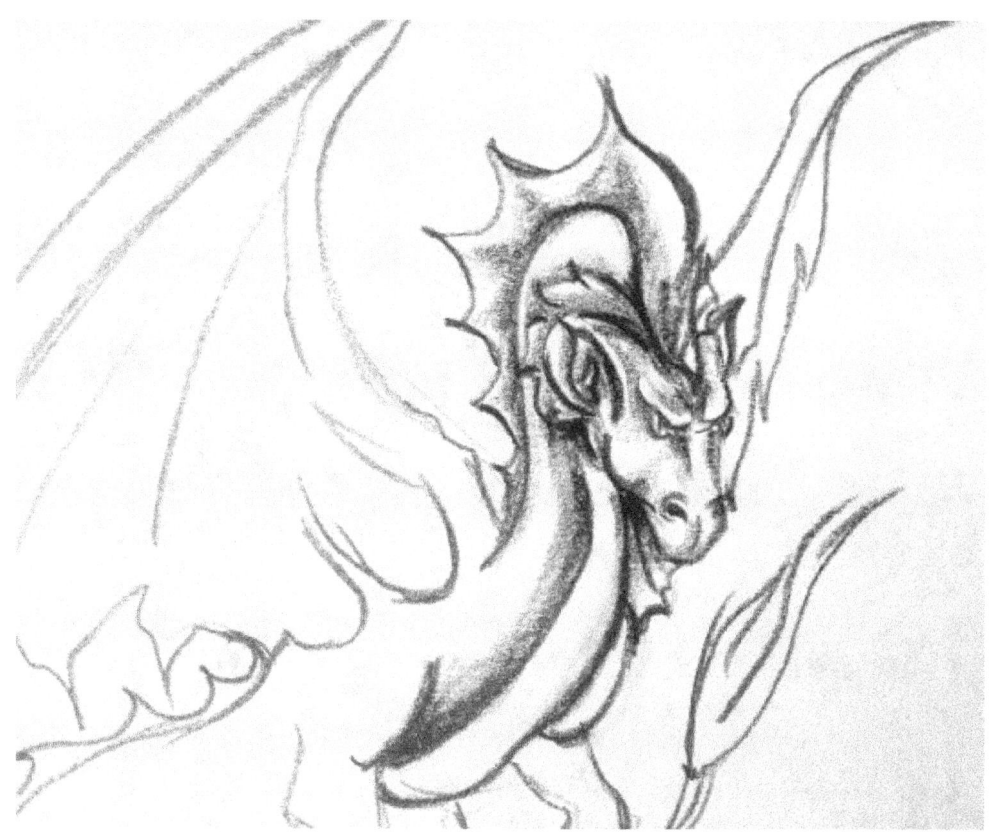

Drawing #4-Extend the shading down the dragon's neck, down towards its belly.

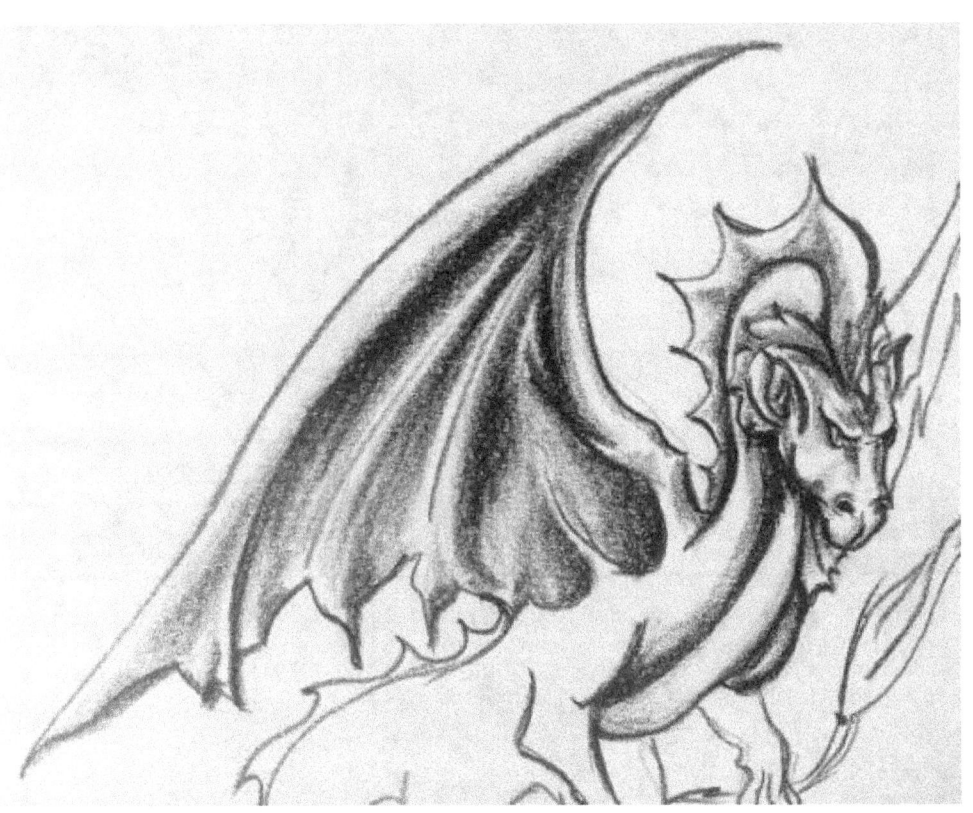

Drawing #5- Shade in the left wing of the dragon. Alternate between areas of white and dark. Put two marks down the middle of the two white triangular regions in the wing.

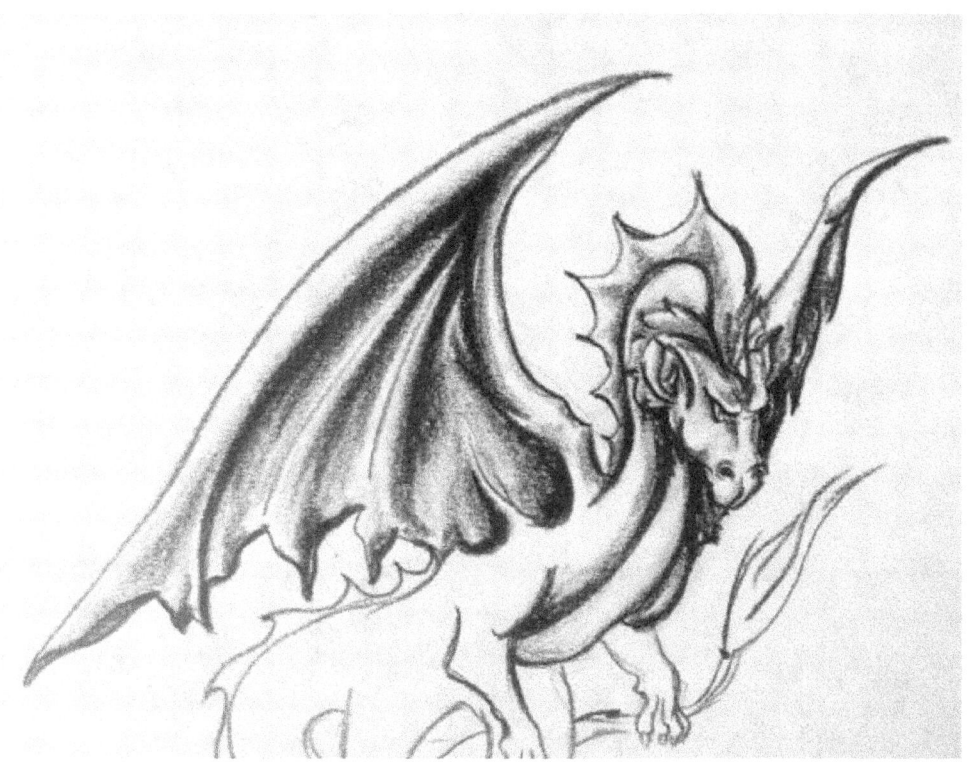

Drawing #6- Make the shading darker on the wing and neck. Add in darker shading along the bottom of the left wing.

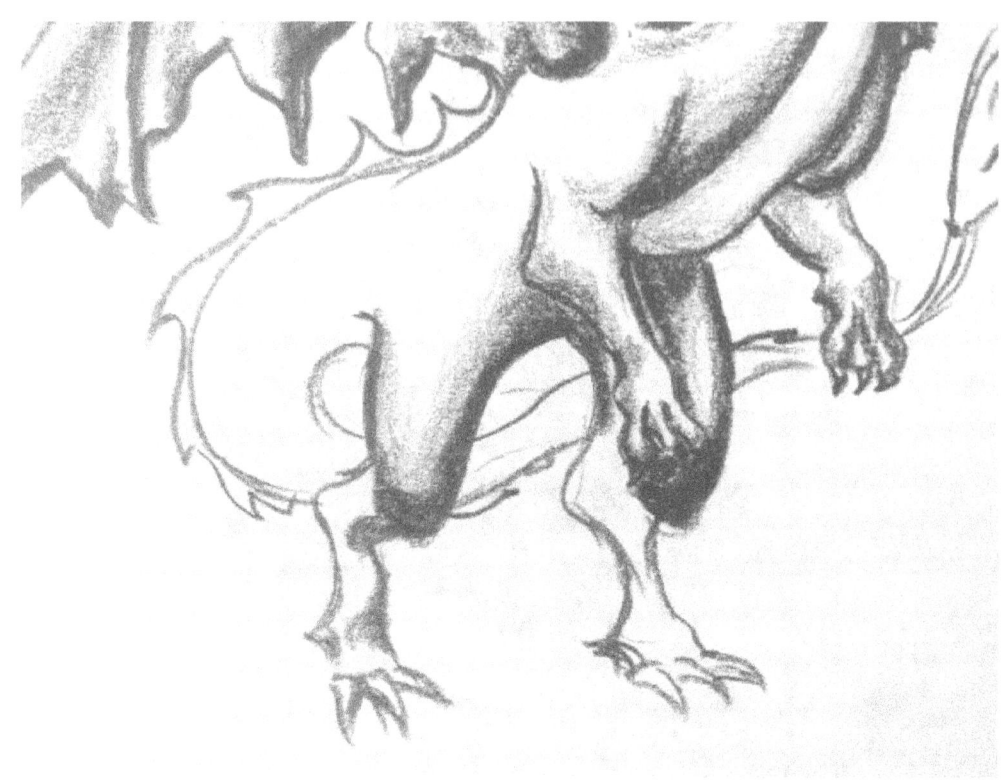

Drawing #7- Shade in knees with really dark shading at the bottom. Make lighter shading above the darker region.

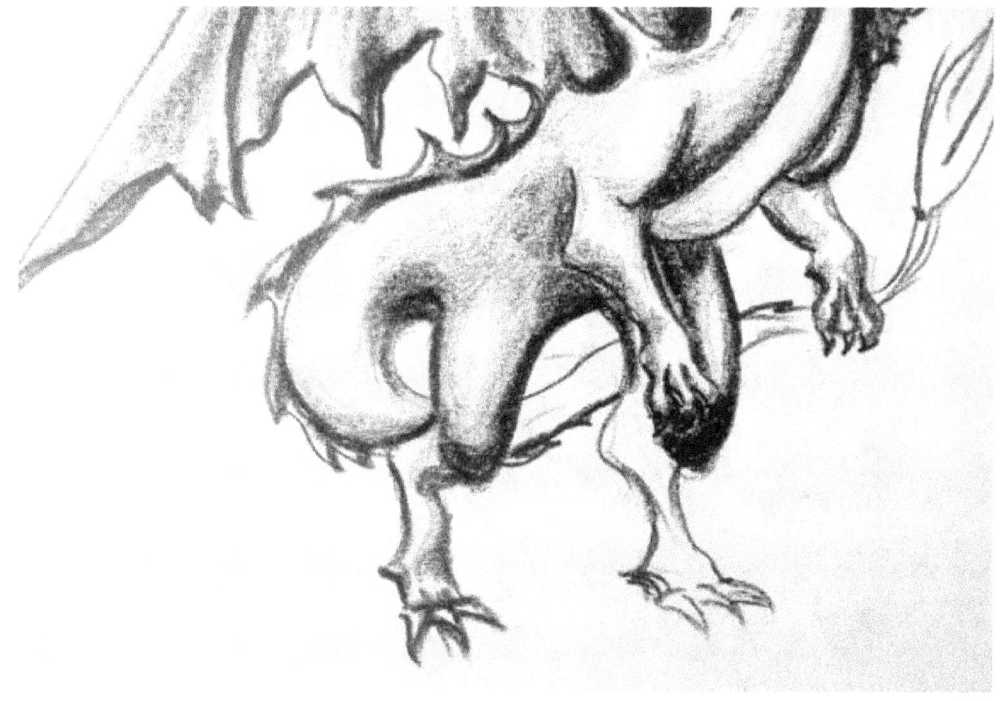

Drawing #8- Add some shading above the left knee that is darker where the body meets the arm and lighter towards the tail.

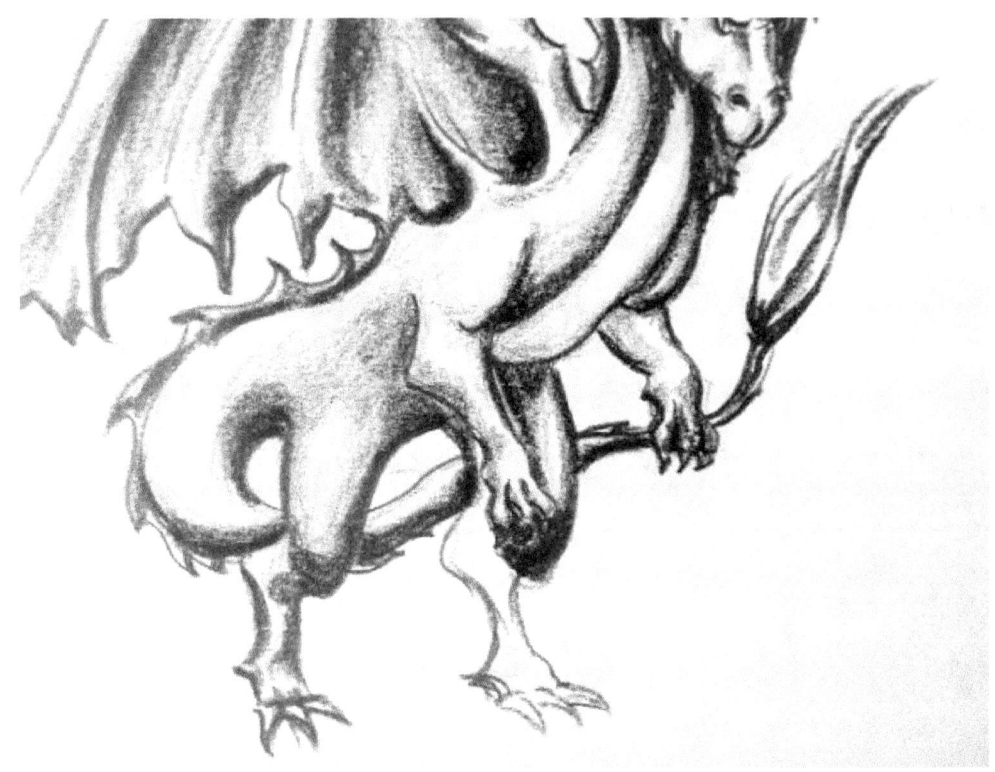

Drawing #9- Along the bottom of the tail, do some darker shading with a little lighter shading above the darker region.

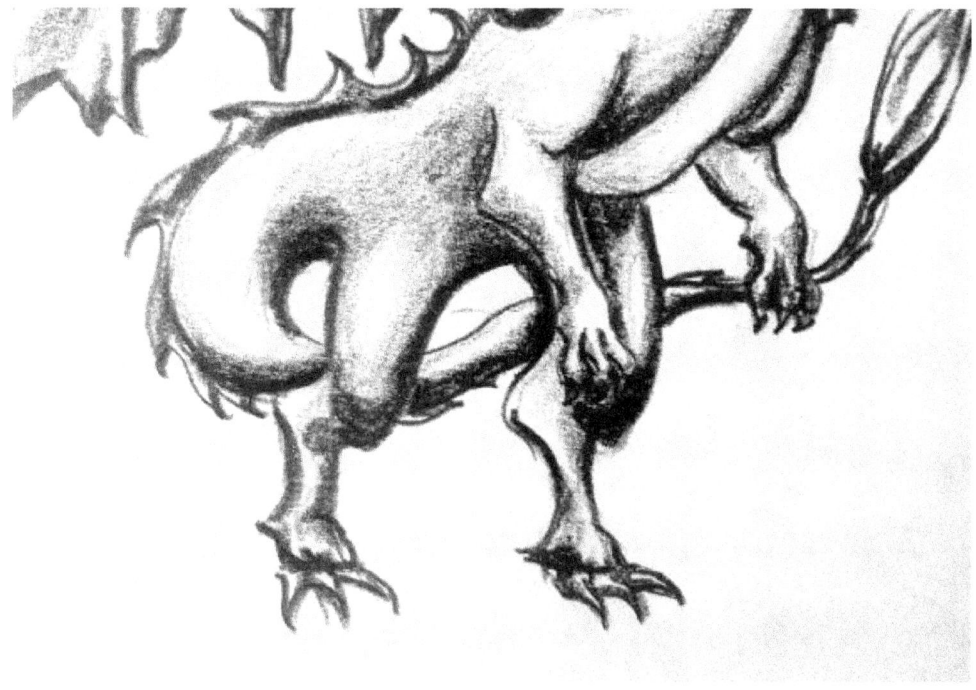

Drawing #10- Draw the outline of the right leg a little darker and use the

side of the pencil to do a little light shading on the top portion of the tail.

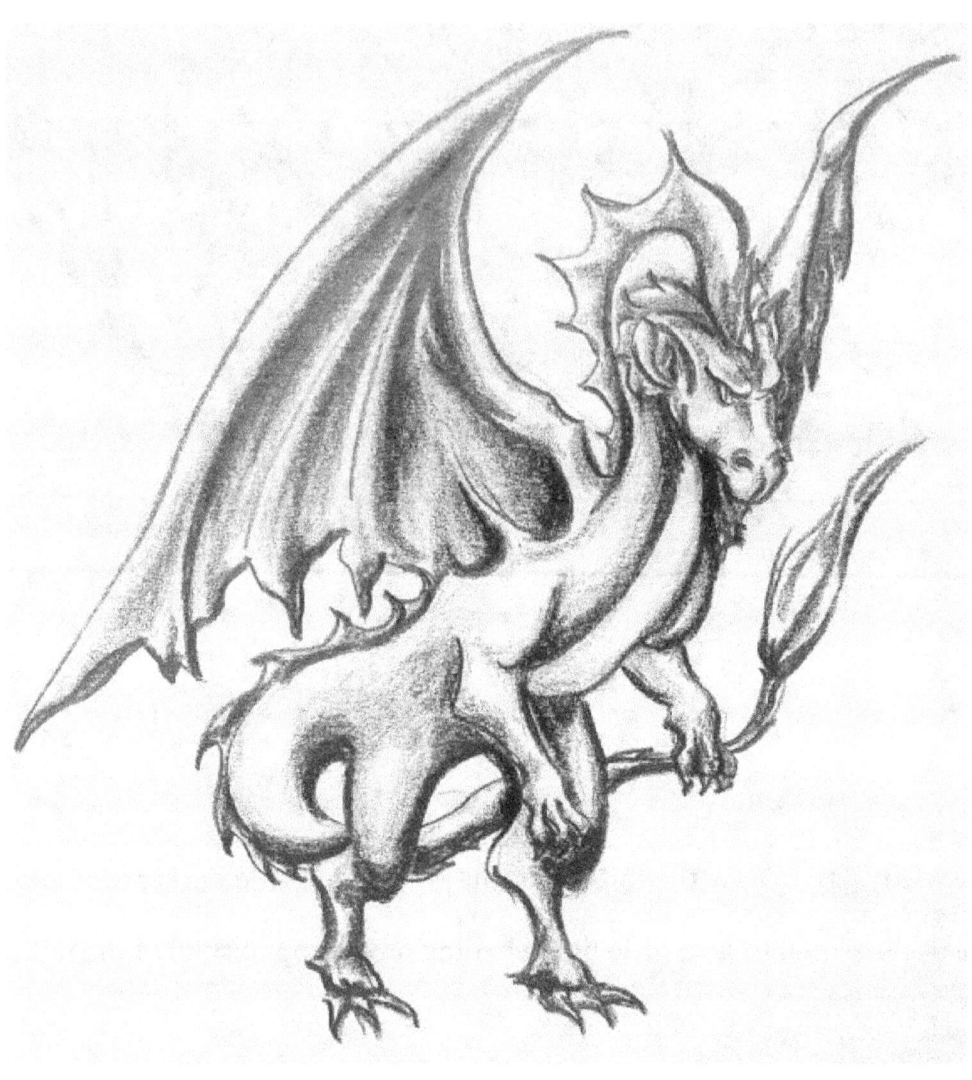

Drawing #11- Here is a full view of what the completed dragon should look like.

Chapter 6– Legless Dragon 2

This dragon resembles the eastern, more serpent-like depiction of the dragon. It does not have the four lizard-like limbs depicted by many of the others. It almost resembles a sea dragon with its feather-like scales.

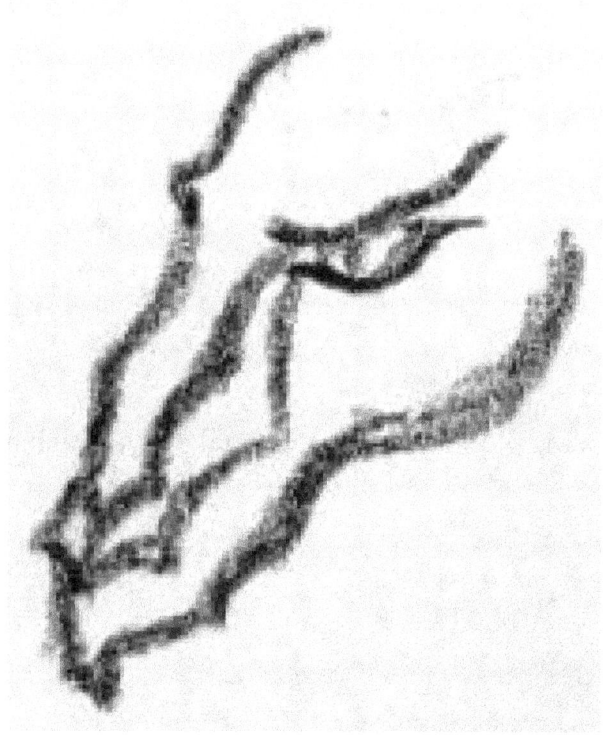

Drawing #1- Use fairly dark marks to make the outline of the dragon's face. Pay special attention to the curves on the outline of the head. Using the drawing as a guideline, make the two markings in the middle of the dragons face with the nostrils on the bottom and the eyebrow the top. Draw in the eye as well.

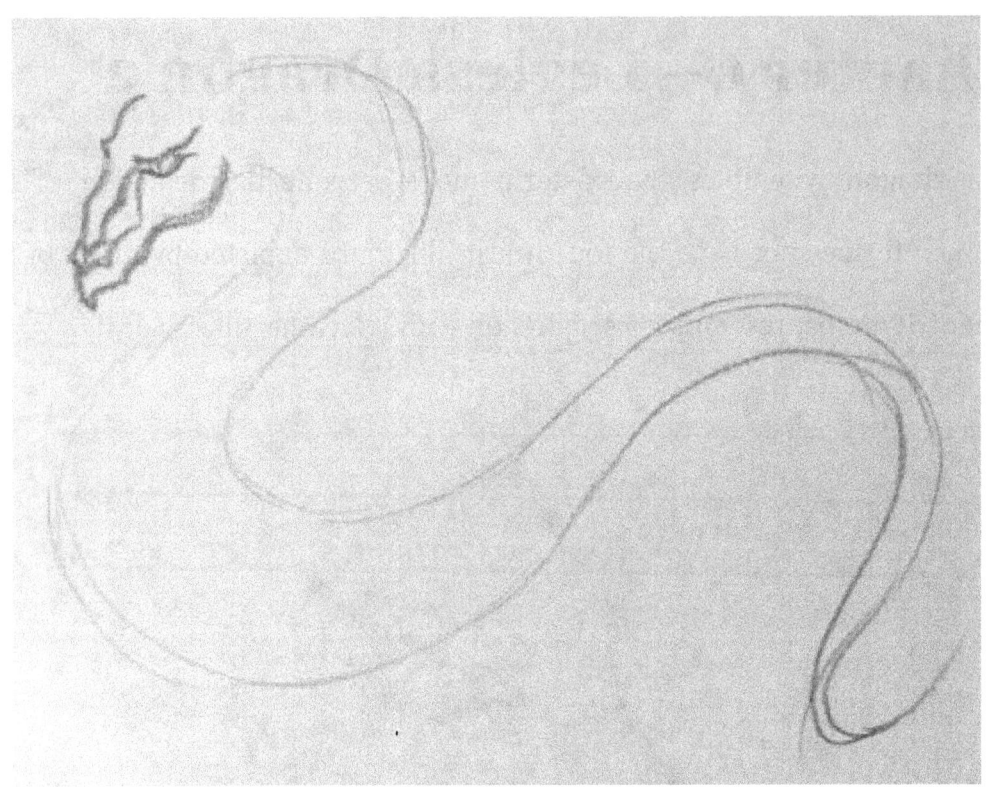

Drawing #2- Using light markings to make the 'S'-shaped body of the dragon.

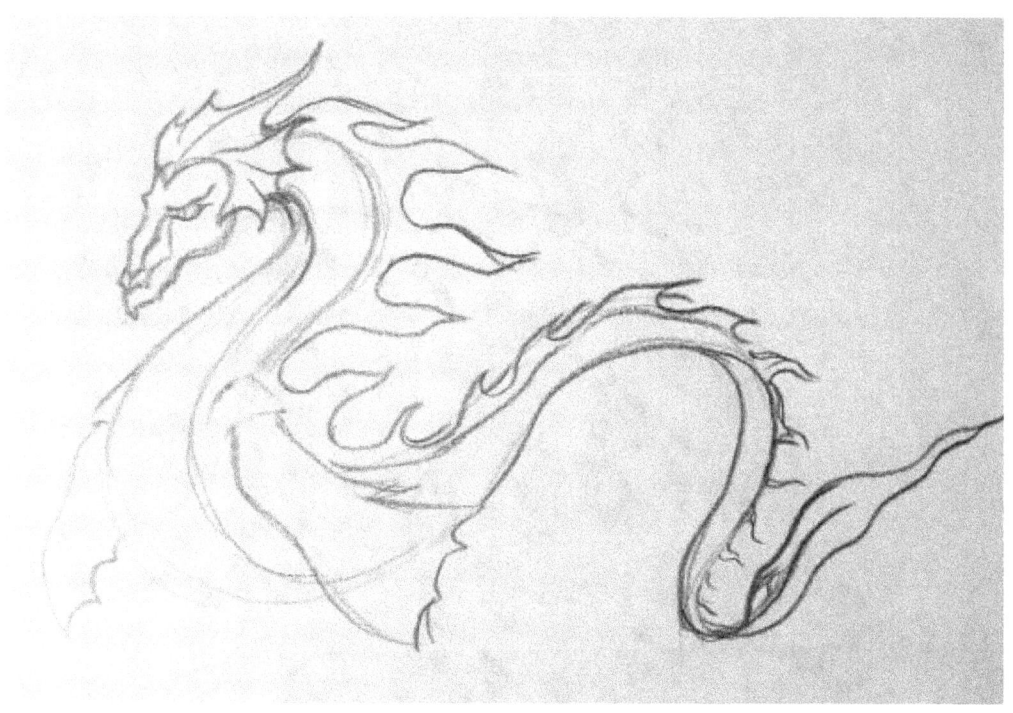

Drawing #3- Draw in the neck frills and pointy scales along the back of the

dragon. Add in the wing shapes at the base of the neck.

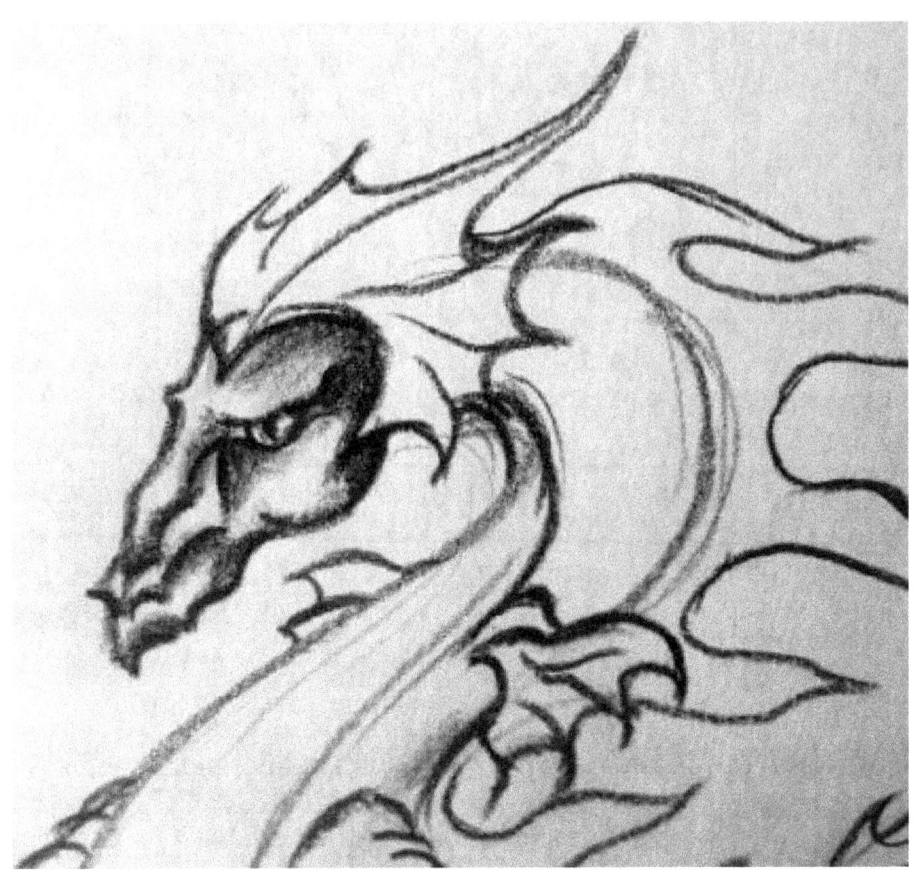

Drawing #4- Go back over the head, frills and wings with bolder strokes. Add some shading in on the face that is fairly dark around the edge of the face and bottom of the chin. Now, put in small wings on either side of the neck. There should be about four points on the right wing.

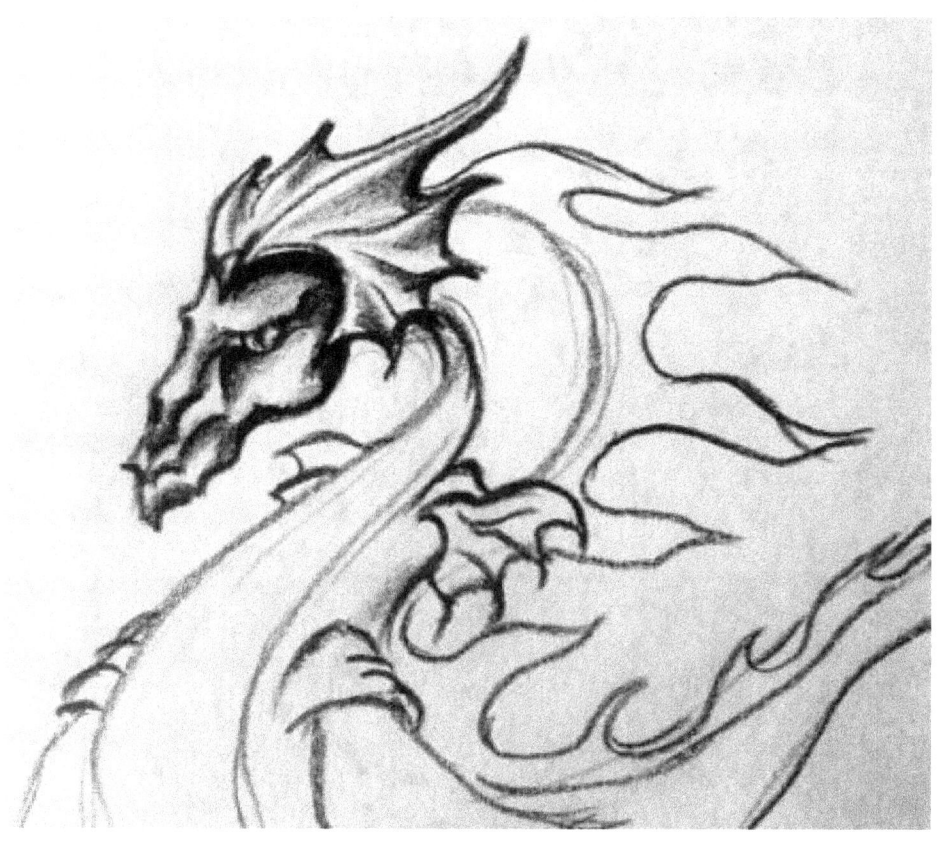

Drawing #5- Put in some shading on the frills on top of the dragon's head with darker shading on the edges and triangular regions of lighter shading radiating from each point.

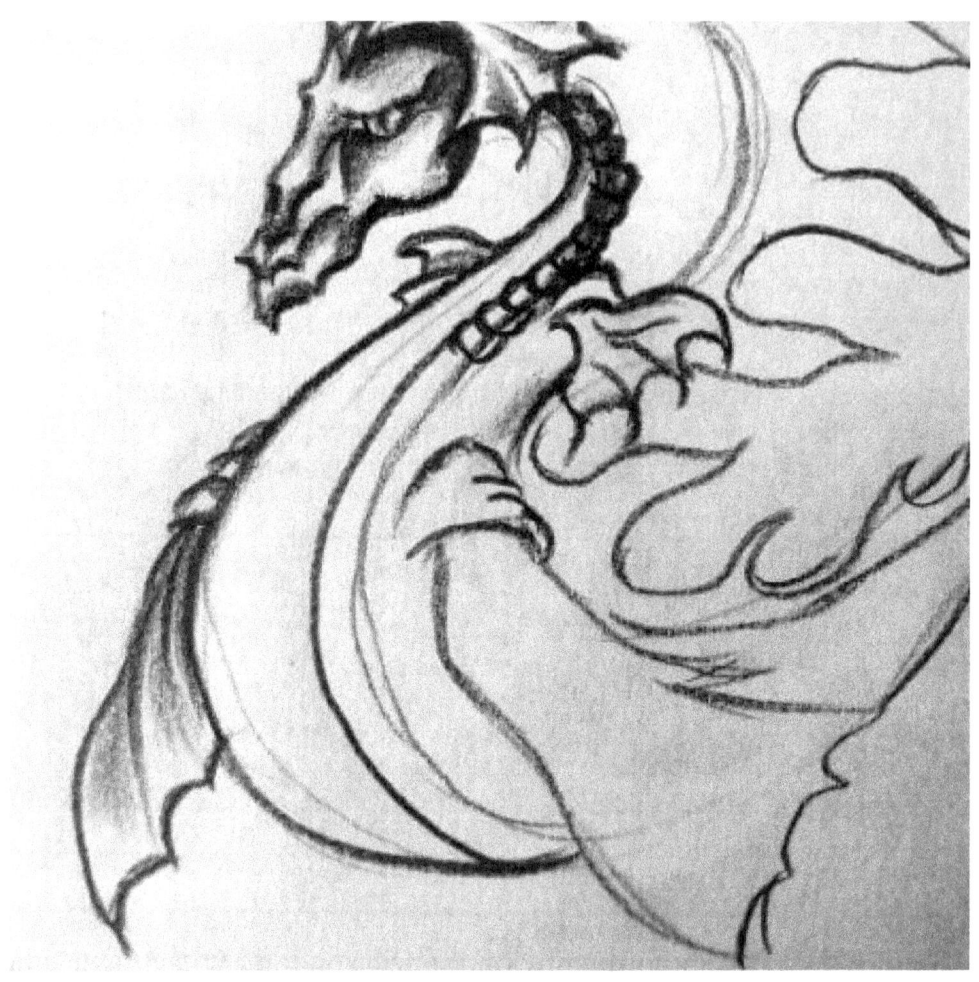

Drawing #6- Begin adding scales on the right side of the dragon's belly extending below the small wings on the neck. Draw in some shading on the left wing.

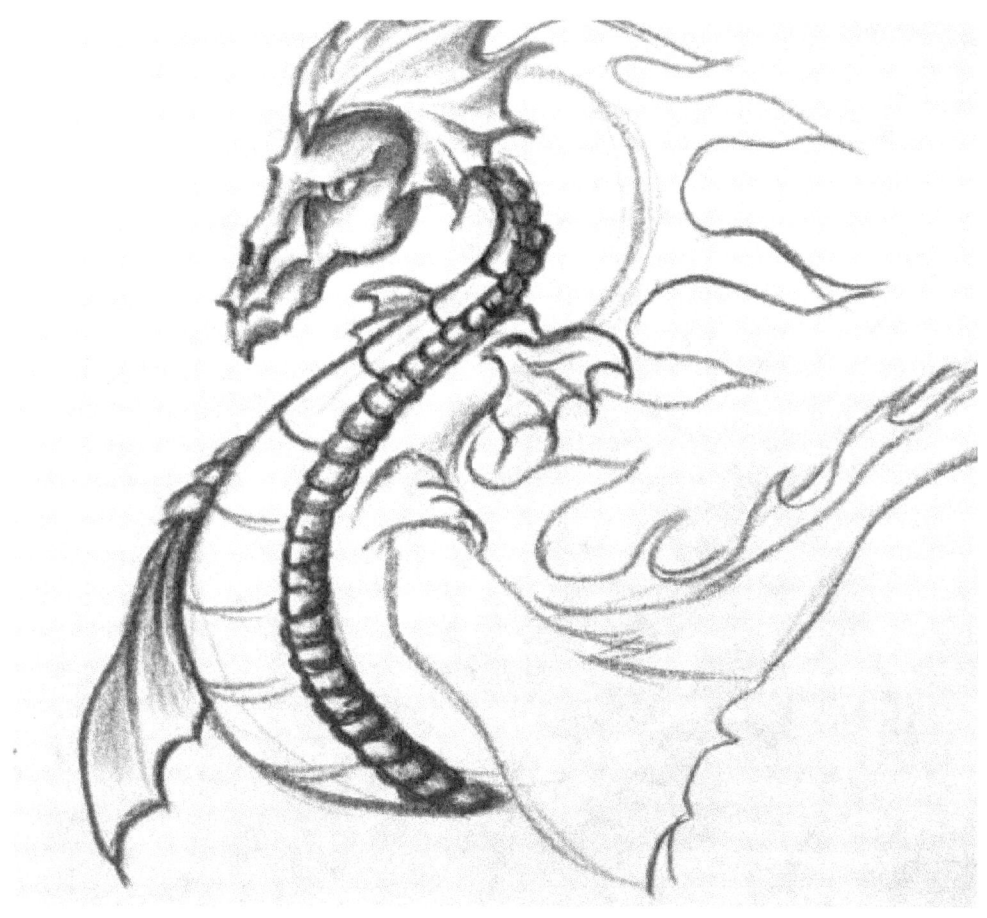

Drawing #7- Put small curved marks all of the way down the dragon's belly. Continue adding the small scales on the right side of the belly extending all of the way down to the bottom of the belly.

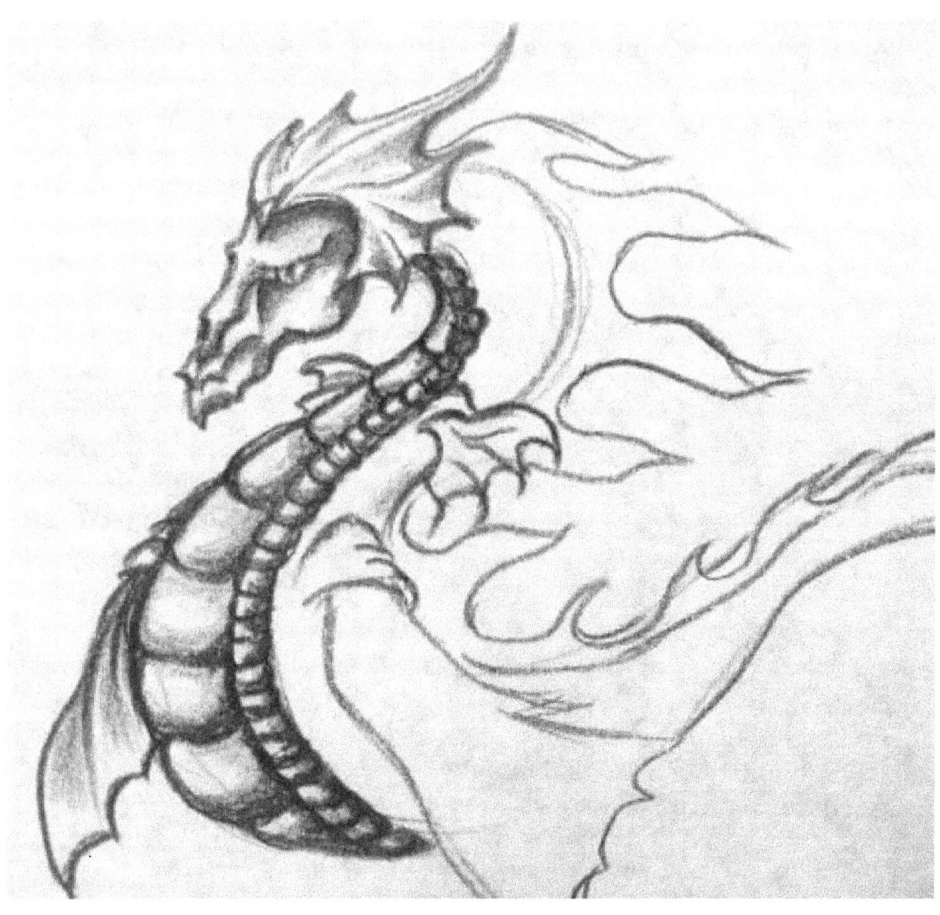

Drawing #8- Add in some shading on the belly of the dragon. Make is dark around the bands on the belly and lighter above them.

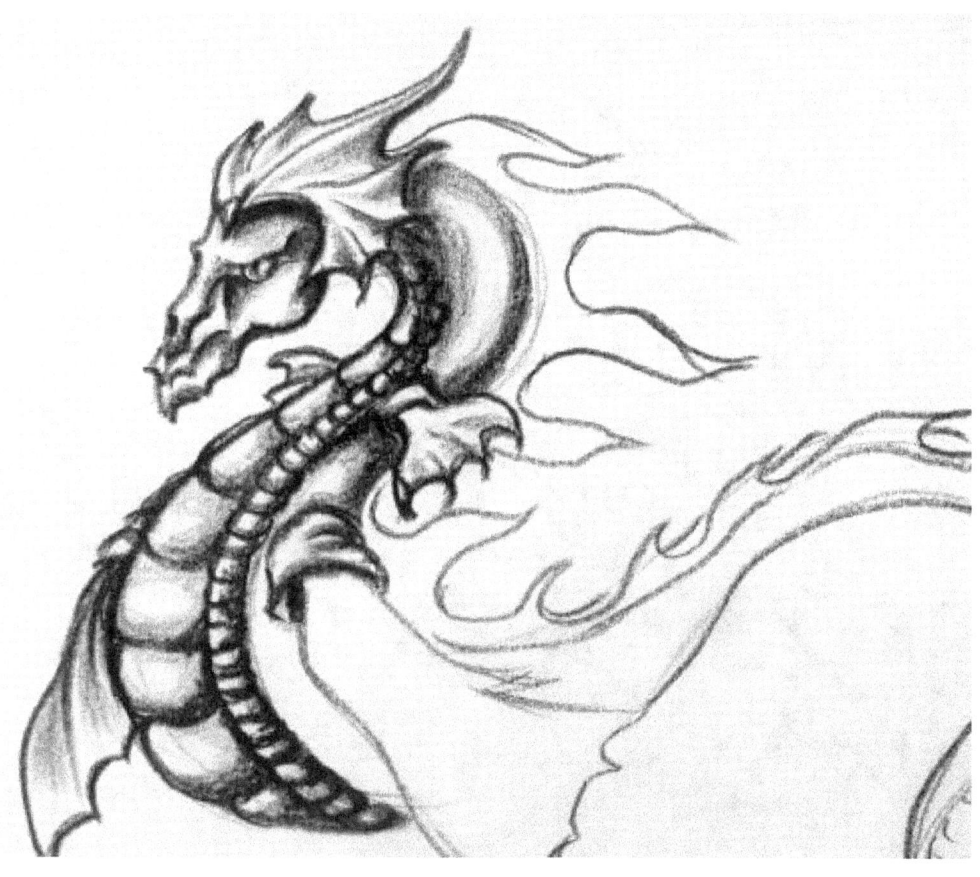

Drawing #9- Draw some darker shading above and below the small right wing along the edges.

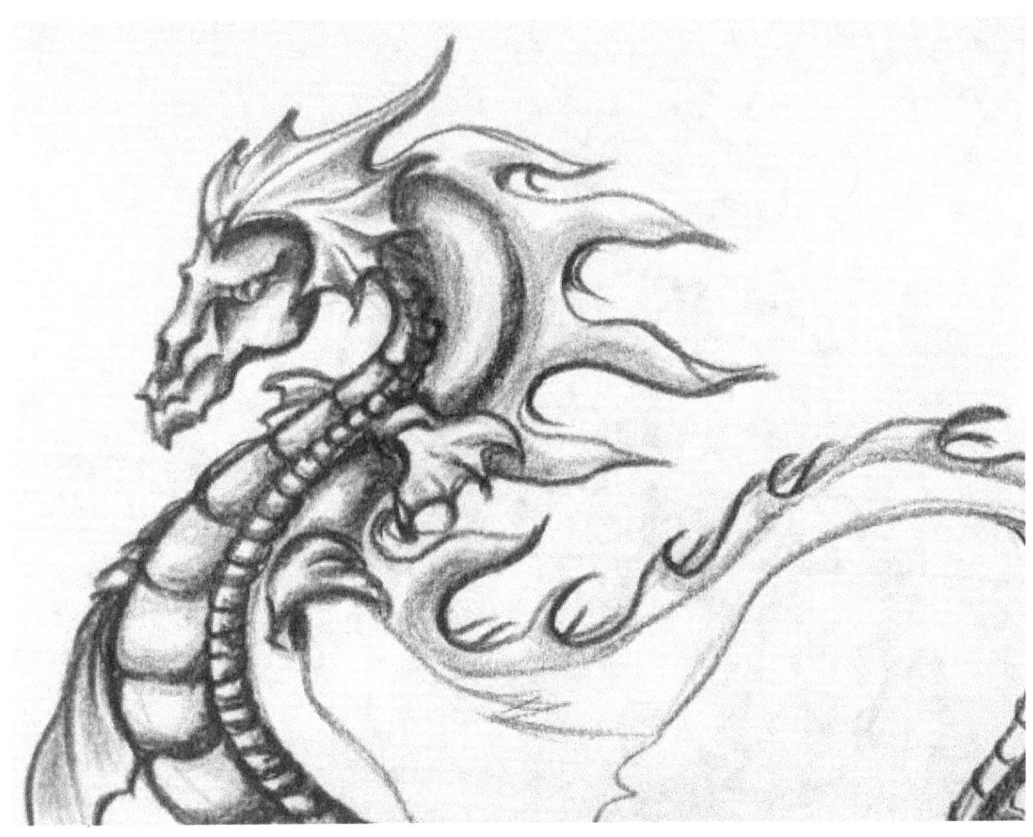

Drawing #10- Add some light shading on the pointy scales that go down the dragon's back. Follow the pattern on the drawing.

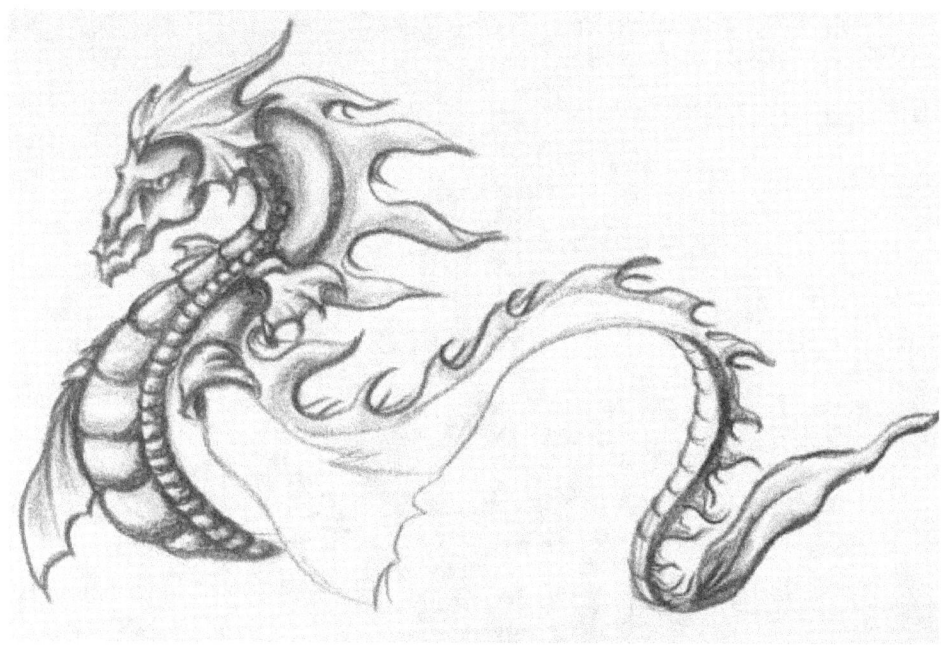

Drawing #11- Continue drawing pointy scales all of the way down the tail of the dragon. Draw in some curved marks on the underside of the end of the tail and a large, leaf-like structure on the end of the tail with a bit of shading on the tip of the tail.

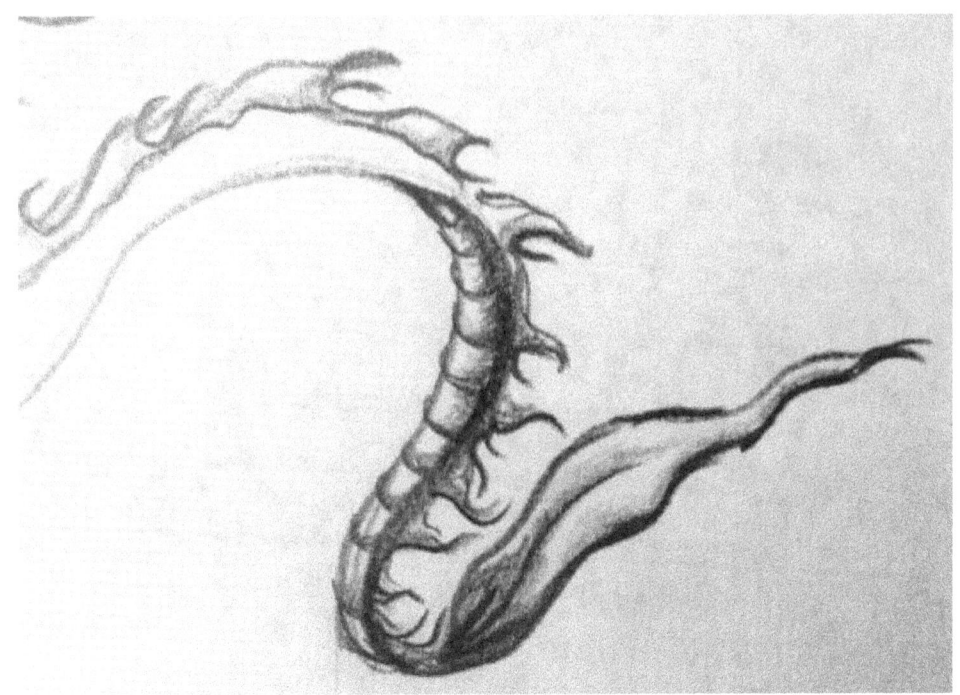

Drawing#12- Add a little more dark shading along the right side of the end of the tail with some lighter shading that extends out from the darker region.

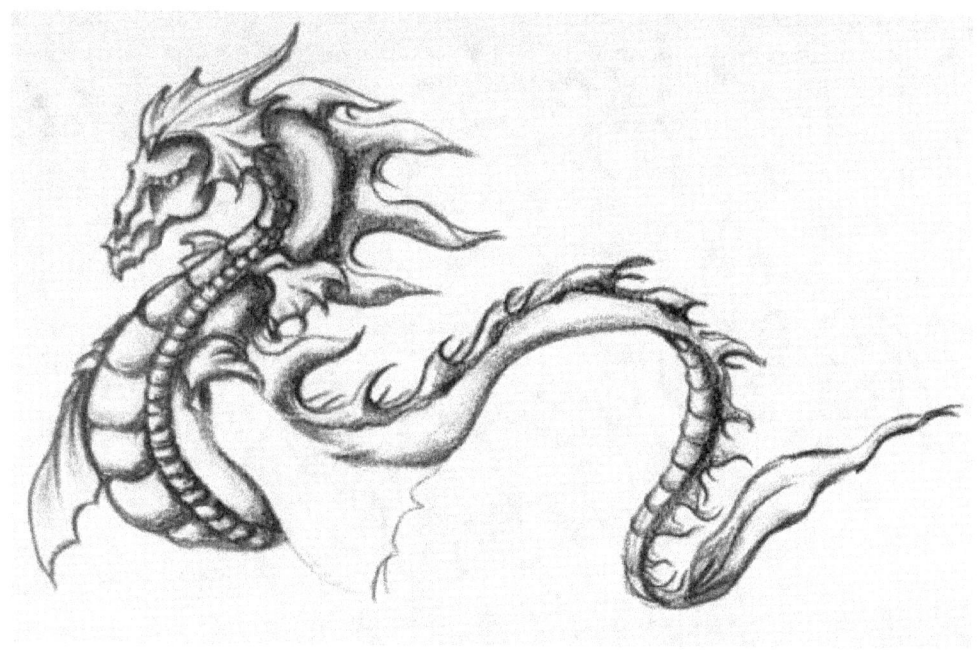

Drawing #13- Draw in some lighter shading along the bottom of the mid-section of the tail.

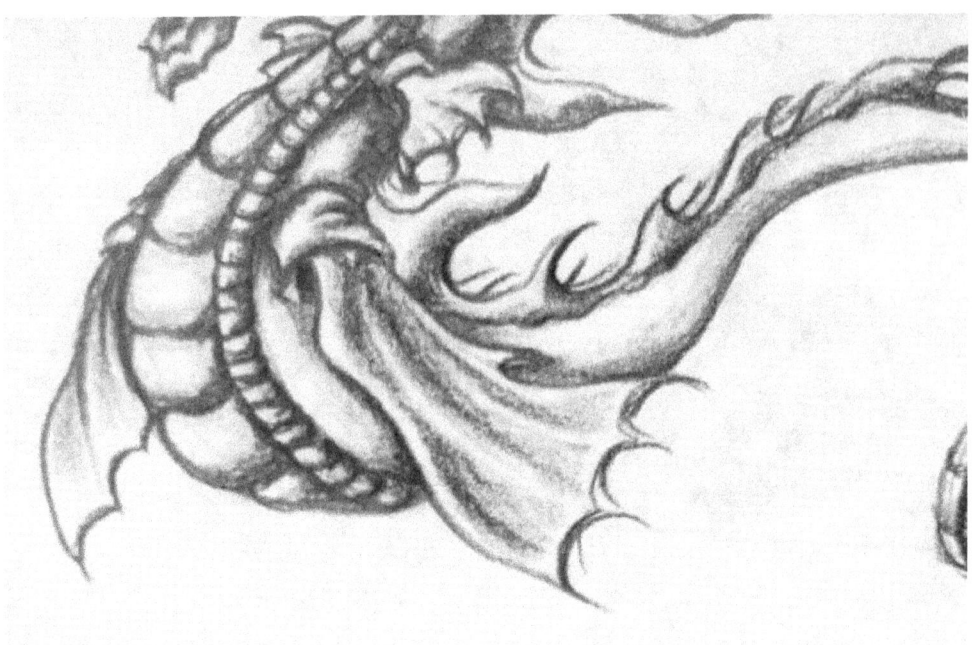

Drawing #14- Now, shade in the right wing with a alternating light and shaded areas. The center portion of each shaded area should be darker than the surrounding shaded region.

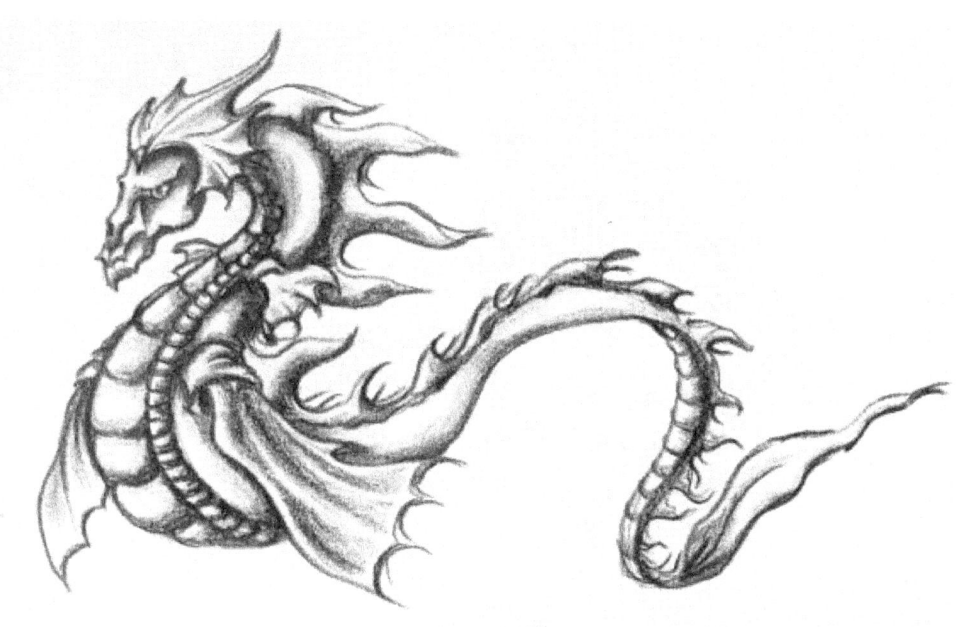

Drawing #15- Here is a shot of the dragon's entire body. You might want to check your drawing now to see if you forgot any shading or marks. Your dragon is complete.

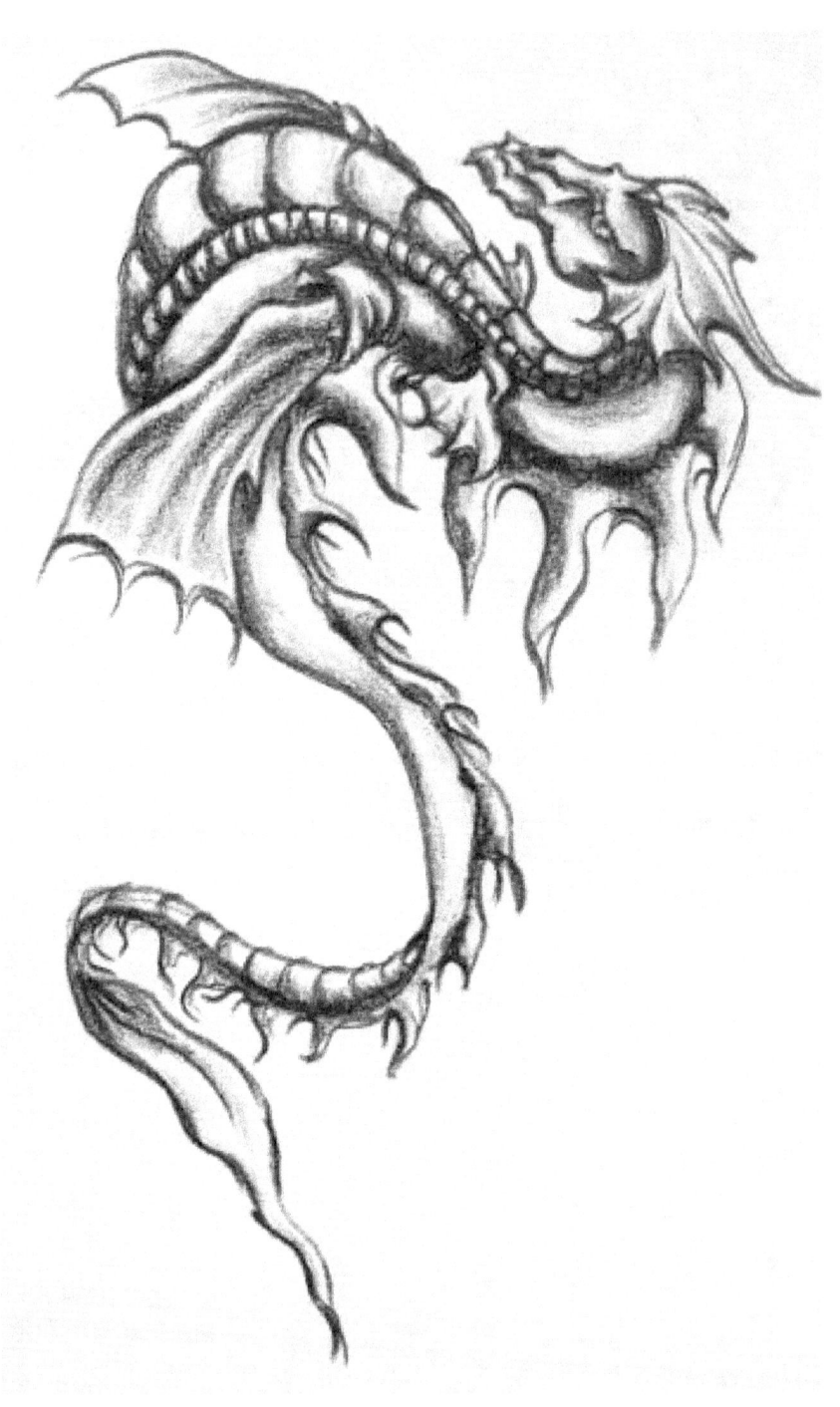

Conclusion

Hopefully, you've become more proficient at drawing dragons after practicing with these six examples. Each one follows a certain pattern that you can use to create your own designs. First, begin with the head of the dragon so that when you draw the body, it will be proportionate to the head. Then, add the limbs, tail, and armor plating. Put in lighter and darker areas of shading to provide some contrast. Once again, using the find point of the pencil to make drawings of the outline of the body and the sides of the pencil for shading. You are sure to be proud of the drawings you have done with the help of this book and all of the other dragon creations that you design in the future!

Thank you!

Thank you for choosing our book, we hope you found it interesting and helpful.

If you liked the book, please give us a favor to write your review.

We would really appreciate this!

If you would like to have a bonus – **FREE BOOK**, please send the screenshot of your review to this e-mail:

kelly.artbooks@gmail.com and we will send you a **FREE BOOK** in PDF as a **GIFT!****

Hope to see you in our future books and good luck in your drawing experience!

** in the e-mail subject please mention the name of the book you reviewed and the author.

www.ingramcontent.com/pod-product-compliance
Lightning Source LLC
Chambersburg PA
CBHW080829180526
45168CB00006B/2625